How to Build A Café Racer

Doug Mitchel

Published by:
Wolfgang Publications Inc.
P.O. Box 223
Stillwater, MN 55082
www.wolfpub.com

Legals

First published in 2013 by Wolfgang Publications Inc.,
P.O. Box 223, Stillwater MN 55082

The information in this book is true and complete to the best of our knowledge. All recommendations are made without any guarantee on the part of the author or publisher, who also disclaim any liability incurred in connection with the use of this data or specific details.

We recognize that some words, model names and designations, for example, mentioned herein are the property of the trademark holder. We use them for identification purposes only. This is not an official publication.

ISBN 13: 978-1-935828-73-0

Printed and bound in U.S.A.

How to Build A Café Racer

Page 7

Chapter Four
Chassis Modifications

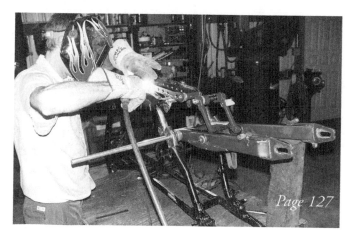

Page 127

Page 38

Dedication

When creating a book of any theme it requires the input and assistance of many outside parties to provide a complete project. In taking on the subject of Café Racers I was forced to go outside my usual band of characters to locate those who had the passion and practical experience of producing the machines or components needed to complete the process. I want to thank the following for their tireless efforts to supply me with facts, images and parts to photograph for use on these pages. The Source Guide found at the back of the book will allow you to find the same people in your quest to complete the Café Racer of your dreams and I highly suggest you contact them for their expertise and guidance.

Steve Baugrud, Joe Bortz, Bob Buckley, Keith Campbell, Randy and Karsten Illg, Brad Powell, John and Terry Rodenhiser, Stew Ross, Ken Rottman, Buzz and Pixie Walneck, Richard Weslow, Air-Tech Streamlining, Analog Motorcycles, Arch Motorcycles, Circle K Kustoms, Coating Specialties, DP Customs, Economy Cycle, Flatland Custom Cycles, Framecrafters, Gustafsson Plastics, JC-Pak Bikes, Ken's British Classics, Motor Cycle Center, Moto-Scoot, Rizoma USA, Streetfighters, Syd's Cycles, Varn Hagen Metalworks, Walneck's Classic Cycle Trader, Zero-Gravity Racing

Have fun and ride safe!

Introduction

It is a well-known fact that riders have been adding personal touches to their motorcycles since the dawn of the industry. Regardless of what genre of machine you ride, no one wants to be seen on a motorcycle like anyone else has. Enhancing performance is another direction the personalization can take and often times both facets of the sport are addressed.

The Café Racer trend began in the latter part of the '50s and really gained momentum in the decades that followed. Early enthusiasts made alterations to their cycles using whatever hardware they could find and used whatever skills they possessed to make the changes. There were not too many avenues for buying parts so the eager rider had to be creative and resourceful to attain the items sought. In today's world we have a vast array of options at our fingertips and can easily secure nearly any part needed to upgrade a motorcycle no matter the brand and model. While the methods of finding what you need have changed the basic instincts to bring about the modifications is rooted deeply in our past.

By choosing to take the path of the Café Racer you are more than likely opting for performance over comfort and riding across the country may not be on your agenda. Of course anyone wanting to do so is free to plan their journey as long as only the barest of essentials are brought along for the trip. Saddle bags, trailers and other means of storing supplies aboard a Café Racer are not frequent and contradict the purpose of the cycles in this class.

Once the decision has been made to alter your existing machine to Café Racer status you'll be faced with a plethora of choices for every segment of the build. Brakes, engine mods, body work and suspension can all be modified with only a modicum of effort. In the event you are not capable of making the wanted upgrades there is also a bevy of shops around the country who are staffed with talented technicians who can do the work on your behalf.

With no rules cast in stone you are faced with a daunting list of choices when converting a motorcycle to Café Racer mode. All we suggest is that safety and mechanical integrity be maintained so you can enjoy the efforts of your creation for years to come. Let your alter ego free and have fun when building and riding your Café Racer creation.

6

Chapter One

History

The History of the Café Racer Motorcycle

Although motorcycles had first made their presence known before the turn of the twentieth century, the act of building custom machines came a bit later. One part of that delay was based on the scarcity of available components to make changes. The initial uses for two-wheeled machines were largely based on commercial or military applications with any modifications tailored to the needs of the end use. Motorcycles pressed into military duty were dressed in appropriate colors and fitted with hardware that met with the objectives of use in the war effort. Industrial and business applications

When speaking of the old days of motorcycling and the infancy of the Café Racer scene it's never long before the Norton Atlas comes up. By combining the traits of the Atlas frame with the strengths of the Norton motor it's easy to see how the juxtaposition came to be. You can find all sorts of variations on the two-brand creations in the history books and the Norton Atlas will always command respect. Photo courtesy of www.bradsbikes.net

were similarly adapted to specific needs often sporting attached storage boxes and related accoutrements.

The trend to alter existing motorcycles in the civilian market was not begun in the states as the youth of Europe had already started building machines to create the new craze. Naturally their chosen machines were native in brand with the British offerings taking the lion's share of the interest. Triumph, BSA, Norton and even a few Vincents found themselves being modified to suit the tastes of the riders. This new menagerie of creativity grew despite the lack of available "bolt-on" upgrades on the market. The use of home spun designs and salvaged materials helped the new-found sport to expand as it required very little money to create a motorcycle that was of your personal taste. Anyone who was handy with a lathe or mill and had access to the machines and raw materials was more than capable of producing unique components aimed at this need and found themselves in demand as other riders sought to add more custom touches to their own mount.

As with any group of people, regardless of their interests, they seek places to meet to exchange tales of glory and often to imbibe in their favorite beverages and foods. In England just such a place gained notoriety amongst the riders of that region. The Ace Café first opened in 1938 and was open 24 hours a day. Its early purpose was to serve vehicles travelling on the newly opened North Circular Road. The round-the-clock operation seemed to draw an unusual amount of motorcycle fans and it quickly became THE place to hang around to discuss your favorite two-wheeled craft and the changes you had made or planned to make. While the Ace Café may have been the primary operation that drew motorcyclists, it wasn't to be the only. England was soon crawling with similar locations that catered to the growing phalanges of motorcycle riders and fans alike. The Busy Bee, Clock Tower, Unicorn and Café Continental were all establishments that were open around the clock and although were not intended for that purpose, drew motorbikes like bees to honey. In their attempts to attract more fans and their families, several of these hot spots offered a youth section so the children had a place to entertain themselves while the grown-ups talked motorcycles. I suppose we are lucky they didn't choose a less desirable location to

Proudly displaying his "59" club patch this Café Racer takes to the roads looking every inch the proper rider involved in the Café Racer scene.

spawn the new facet of the hobby since "Outhouse racer" doesn't carry the same cache.

The "café" name stuck and soon many of the patrons of the Ace Café and other locations earned reputations as devotees to the art of racing.

Granted, not all of the competition was done on authorized venues as the streets in and around London seemed to be adequate to prove who was the fastest. "Doing the ton" was soon adopted as a popular catch-phrase that meant reaching a speed of 100 miles per hour. The combination of the "café" name and the "racer" actions of the enthusiasts soon became the common moniker for anyone seen on a motorcycle, at least in the London area.

The Ace Café was destroyed in an air raid during WW II and rebuilt in 1949. It was not the only establishment to be destroyed during the war as every facet of life was changed by the conflict. Soon after the war ended new buildings were erected, allowing riders fresh spots to regroup. By 1969 new regulations and taxation within England had hampered the operation and profits at the Ace Café forcing the owner little choice but to cease operation of the iconic hangout. It would be many years later when Mark Wilsmore and some business partners wanted to reopen the location seeing the ongoing interest in the Café Racer scene. The spot was opened again in 1997 and by 2001 had returned to its former glory as the place to go when astride your motorcycle. Large gatherings of two-wheeled fun can be found there nearly every weekend and special events draw in even bigger groups of riders. Although not the exact business it once was the newly opened Ace Café would see its history live on for years to follow.

As these "café racers" began to develop a style of their own it became clear that certain modifications were mandatory to keep up with the crowd. In the performance category, exhaust and suspension was the most obvious choices for any rider serious about the craft. Alterations to handlebars, foot pegs and cosmetics typically followed as every rider sought ways to individualize his motorbike. Those who were lucky enough to make internal motor modifications did so but many were limited to more readily available technology and scrap materials of the day. As time rolled on, upgrades were made to the appearance of the machines with the addition of solo saddles, fiberglass fairings and polished components adding to the gleam of the cycles. Custom paint schemes were often added to spice up the variety and soon there was no end

While on his spirited ride it appears that this rider is checking his gauges to ensure safe operation of his cycle. His German NSU from 1956 is proof that nearly any machine can be turned into a Café Racer.

to what changes could be made to personalize your own machine, as long as your intentions were to look good and go faster.

The 1950s brought numerous improvements to the world of motorcycling in England. The variety of brands and models began to grow along with bank financing for the purchase of your dream machine. 1950 saw the end of gas rations as well providing ample fuel to motivate the further expansion of the hobby. As history got deeper into the '50s and '60s there were those who couldn't be satisfied with anything a single brand could offer and began melding two different marques into a single creation. "Triton" (Triumph and Norton), "Norvin" (Norton and Vincent) and "Tribsa" (Triumph and BSA) were the more common blends of well-known brands with several lesser-known variants found prowling the streets of England. The Norton featherbed chassis, designed by Rex McCandless was the first choice for any rider seeking to add some racing heritage and performance into his Café creation. The first sanctioned race that the Norton featherbed frame was entered in, achieved a win, setting the reputation for the design in stone.

It wasn't long after the post-war buildings were finished when groups of riders known as "Mods" and "Rockers" began to form and hold court.

Without delving into the entire history of the two groups, the "Rockers" were typically seen aboard their motorcycles in black leather jackets, unkempt hair styles and were devotees to the rock and roll universe. The "Mods" dressed in stylish suits and ties, neatly coifed hair, rode custom scooters and leaned towards the jazz end of the musical empire. Their conflicts became larger as each segment grew and a few storied clashes made the record books. 1964 saw a clash between the two groups that resulted in numerous arrests but no one

was injured in the scuffle. Other splinter groups of riders were also formed as themes of garb and riding styles began to diversify as the numbers of riders increased. Despite their many differences, members of the groups remained fairly true to the original "Café Racer" format, at least as far as their motorcycles were concerned.

Another faction of the Café Racer scene was Club 59 which started in 1959 and was designed to give some younger children a better path than the ones they had begun to travel. Started by two religious figures that were also cycle enthusiasts, they delivered their words to those they felt could benefit from a more positive influence. The classic "59" logo remains popular today and can be seen on patches sewn onto jackets and vests no matter where you travel in the motorcycle world.

Once the Second World War was over, soldiers returning home to the USA had an insatiable appetite for motorcycles as a pure form of entertainment. Many had been given their first taste riding motorcycles during their time in the service and had enjoyed the experience. Harley-Davidson and Indian were the two marques often ridden during the conflicts and therefore chosen as mounts when returning to American soil. Upon their return home they found a large number of surplus military motorcycles offered for sale at a bargain basement price. Once buying the machines, plans to modify the cycles began in earnest.

Some of the first stateside alterations were called choppers because the owners would simply chop off any component that weighed too much or was considered excessive. This form of custom building led to bobbers that also had sections of fenders removed for performance reasons or just to improve appearance. Neither of these forms of the early customs was true to the Café formula but as time went by, the riders in the USA were drawn to

It wasn't long after the post-war buildings were finished when groups of riders known as "Mods" and "Rockers" began to form and hold court.

the sleek designs and enhanced output of the café machines. As alterations grew in popularity even the U.S. riders began choosing British machines as the platforms for their next Café Racer. The forms and hardware of the British marques lent themselves to a truer Café creation and allowed the overseas brands to gain acceptance and recognition in the states. Components required to modify your machine whether domestic or imported remained a fairly sparse commodity but as in the early days those with the skills and gear could turn out some terrific parts for that use. Government regulations were not as strict as today's allowing greater flexibility in the alteration of equipment but also provided some riders to go beyond what was safe in their efforts to look the part and enhance performance. After racking up enough injuries and deaths, steps

were taken to limit what was legal to change but even today we see people pushing that envelope to the limit and beyond.

In the last few years the Café Racer scene has grown to new levels in the U.S. and that desire and enthusiasm has seen a range of companies being formed to supply the needed bits and services to build these stylish and competitive motorcycles. Every facet of the machine can be addressed and altered to your specific needs and all you need to do is spend some time on the internet to locate and buy what you seek. Of course you can still wander at local swap meets to find what you need and both options are viable and offer their own brand of effort. In doing research for this book I was amazed at how many firms are now in existence to cater to nothing but the Café market. Bodywork, motor

The performance theme of the XLCR was enhanced by a pair of disc brakes. Note the, cafe fairing and - unique to this model - tank, seat and tail section. The dark color was accented by a few traces of gold. Cast wheels added some additional flair to the sporty machine. Sadly the Café Racer from Milwaukee didn't catch on with Harley buyers and it would only be on the roster for one year after the machine rolled into view.

components and a wide array of trim upgrades can be found on today's market and should fill every need you can create. There are also a growing number of builders who cater to the rider who has no desire or skill to assemble their own machine but still have the desire to participate in the arena and attend local events.

Overseas we still find a much bigger group of people taking part in the hobby and many tap into the decades of history that was born at their feet. Having been around at the start of the sport or at least been exposed to it as a youth, they have deep-seated roots and continue to illustrate their enthusiasm for that segment of the two-wheeled world.

As we see in many different types of hobbies, the basic premise on which it began often changes as it travels down its path. In the custom motorcycle universe we have witnessed the birth of the radical choppers in the '60s and '70s only to see them reborn in the early part of the new millennium. When they began to reappear at that point in time they took on new levels of sophistication and even more extreme dimensions. That segment of the timeline was brief but brought the rest of the world in focus with what had been going on for years if not decades. I am willing to bet that the Café Racer scene will also go through some permutations as it travels ahead into the future. More radical modifications will be seen and variations of those will appear as people learn from others in their quest for personal perfection. It will be entertaining to see what the next wave of Café Racers is, who will be building them and what levels of science and creativity will be brought into the fold.

The XLCR made its debut as a 1977 model and was a radical departure from other models sold by Harley. The blacked-out paint scheme extended to the Siamese exhaust and continued to the sport fairing and sleek tail section. The shape and concept were new for Harley as they hoped to gain some traction on the expanding Café Racer excitement of the period.

Chapter Two

Goals

Goals for Your Café Racer

Before you select an acceptable machine and begin turning the wrenches you need to determine how you'll use your Café Racer once it's completed. As you will often read in this book there are no wrong answers to this question. Even though there are no rules about what you can do, there are obvious methods to do any alteration correctly to ensure safe operation when completed. Saving a few dollars on a bargain part may make sense or be your only option a certain day but it is usually better to wait until you can secure the best components you can find before bolting them in

This creation, owned by Steve Baugrud, blends fairly current capabilities of a 2006 Suzuki Savage with the throwback appearance of the RYCA CS-1 bodywork. Landing on the line between Café Racer and flat track machine this example still works great regardless of which view you take.

place. Not only will this deliver you a far better end result but in the event you need to sell your machine later you'll have nothing to make excuses for.

Obviously a basic understanding of a motorcycle's operation is required and a license to ride the machine in your state comes in handy. Beyond those two basics guidelines the rest is an open book awaiting your own creativity. By adhering to the guidelines set down by manufacturers and builders you'll be far more certain of creating a Café Racer that will bring years of thrills with a minimum of disappointment.

Steve opted to powder coat the single-cylinder 652cc engine in black to contrast with the copper hue and to compliment the accent stripe which is also black.

Two of the more distinct riding options would be riding or racing. There may be some who plan on doing a little of both so that too will need to be addressed before making a purchase. Simple pleasure rides around your neighborhood or the country doesn't ask your machine to do the things demanded of a race machine and for the most part vice-versa. While you might be able to enjoy a race-bred machine on the streets, one designed for tooling around town will not suffice under harsh racing conditions. Most motorcycles built for purely racing events won't even be street legal when considering noise and lighting laws in your state. If you've ever attended a large motorcycle rally you might be surprised at the volume some machines pro-

A pair of clip-on bars are matched with Joker Machine concealed bar-end mirrors for an aggressive rider posture and great rear vision.

Using a piece of Triumph's catalog offerings, this rider has converted it to meet with racing regulations and can now ride safely on the track. Note the Café rear section and lower bars.

The rider aboard this copy has gone to more extreme levels with the addition of the full coverage fairing and modifying the running gear to more specific specs.

The RD series from Yamaha continues to be a popular choice by street and track riders alike as we see here an RD350 on course at Road America.

duce even though they are street legal. Obviously certain types of "racing" can be achieved by two-wheeled crafts on the road but are probably frowned upon by the law enforcement segment of the population. It is also not a safe way to enjoy the performance of your cycle so try to keep others in mind before taking your lunacy to the streets.

A FEW CHOICES THAT CAN DO EITHER

When deciding whether to keep your riding on the street or go to the track there are a few choices that do both, just not at the same time. As you'll soon read, modifying a cycle for purely race use will require removing several components and functions that are crucial to the street legal craft. The same goes for a race machine as to do either task well there will be some changes that make them unsuitable for the other. Before choosing to go racing you may want to spend some time on the road gaining confidence and learning the important yet very basic rules of riding a motorcycle. If you later choose to head to the track there are a handful of cycles that can be equipped for both and may save you some grief and money down the road.

Later in this book you'll see a few examples of cycles that began life as factory machines and were then converted to the café racer mold.

Honda's CB200 is one example with images of both varieties in these pages. The Yamaha RD series is another classic model that can suit your needs on the street or track. From Italy we also see some of Ducati's efforts being used on both venues and looking great regardless of their destination. BMW offers a few iconic models that too can be modified for action on the track. In the Triumph faction you can find vintage and modern copies of their machines being used at every corner of riding adventures. Limiting your choices to only two-cylinder examples from Triumph will still open the door to contemporary and vintage realms. You'll also find a great selection of parts for either slice of history when going the British way.

Some choices may be capable of doing track and street time but you will also find that when pushed to perform at track levels many of the choices fall flat at competitive venues but can still be vastly entertaining on the street. As always, shop carefully review the choices and talk to the experts before putting down your hard earned money.

PLANS TO BUILD A STREET MACHINE

As we already know there are few fixed rules when it comes to building a Café Racer for your own use. When choosing to assemble or create a motorcycle that will never do anything more than ride around town or even the open road you are faced with choices and restrictions. The restrictions tend to be dictated by state, city and county guidelines. A certain noise level must be attained as well as proper lighting and tire choices. Depending on the state you reside in, eye and head protection must be reviewed and taken into consideration too but they pertain to anyone riding a motorcycle not just the Café rider. Of course comfort should be taken into review as well as you'd rather enjoy your time aboard your cycle, not hate every mile.

The majority of cycles built for street use will never see a dirt road or unpaved surface so tire choice is easier to make. Odds are you wouldn't take a true Café Racer onto a gravel or dirt surface by choice anyway so that will also dictate the rubber chosen.

Even staying within the "street tire" classification you will find an enormous quantity of available brands, tread styles and appearance. In your efforts to build and ride a machine that will be both safe and pleasant to ride I suggest you turn to a tire expert to assist you in your choices. You can find these talented folks by turning to catalogs whether online or in print. They can easily suggest a tire that will best suit your planned riding style and help steer you to a suitable installation as well. Many street bound tires include a high mileage number which will allow you to travel for many years on one set of rubber based entirely on your annual distance. This group of tires will also handle admirably in wet conditions while providing a good level of comfort. The overall dimensions of your chosen tires must also work with your plans for fenders and required clearance for safe opera-

Another example of a race bred Café Racer is taken to the track at Road America and is one of many that day that bring the thrill of racing to the level they feel comfortable.

Perhaps not as common as the Café Racers built with British or Japanese machines, the BMW line is often tapped for conversion as we see with this 80/7.

There may be no big money at stake at the vintage races but the riders take to the action with no lack of intensity and passing is common.

tion. Choosing a larger diameter tire might increase the footprint the rubber makes with the road but still must fit properly to your stock or aftermarket rims. Once installed be sure that the tires and wheels function properly within the tubes of the swingarm and front fork as well.

All of these parameters need to be taken under consideration before buying and mounting the tires that fit your design. Choosing form over function never ends well on a moving vehicle especially one without the protection provided by a roof, doors and seat belts.

In the appearance department you are faced with numerous options as well. Blackwall, raised white letters or white walls are all among the varying direction you can take. Adding up tire size, tread and design will more than likely provide you with a list that will need to be whittled down before you take out your checkbook.

Whether you choose to use the factory rims or locating a set found on the aftermarket you will once again be faced with a myriad of choices to make. If staying with the factory rims they will need to be inspected to ensure they are not bent, dented or out of round. Bent spokes will also need

to be replaced with proper components to deliver a safe and reliable base for your new tires. The choices in replacement rims will depend largely on the type and brand of cycle you choose to create your Café Racer from. A majority of aftermarket wheels come in a choice of alloys, saving weight and adding some flair to the overall design. Some that can be ordered with a finish other than chrome including some very interesting anodized hues or a colorful paint or powder coat surface. Modern powder coating can be had in a huge variety of colors and shades every one of which provides a really durable, long lasting finish. Powder coating can be applied to any metal that can withstand a temperature of 400 degrees leaving nearly every alloy within your grasp. A few softer metals will not be allowed but they would be too soft to use as a wheel rim to begin with, thus making their choice a non-issue.

A big selection of high performance braking components can be found in today's aftermarket, including both new rotors and multi-piston calipers. Be sure you understand the basic physics of brakes before buying the new components so you get the most braking power for the buck.

Generally more is better, more rotor area and more caliper pistons pushing bigger brake pads. Remember that replacing the front caliper(s) means paying attention to the diameter of the master cylinder piston. The hydraulic ratio needs to be considered so the master cylinder has enough volume to move the caliper pistons, while at the same time generating enough power to ensure good solid stops.

The CB200 from Honda is a common choice for racer and street rider and this example is fully decked out for track time.

Some of these brake upgrades are bolt on, while others will require new or custom brackets. At this point it's a good idea to find a capable and experienced shop, both to ensure the components you buy will match up with any remaining factory components (like the master cylinder) and also for help with the actual installation. Safely is key here, don't skimp on parts, and if in doubt about your mechanical abilities go ahead and pay the shop to do the install correctly.

Depending on what year, make and model you have chosen for Café Racer use you may be able to improve the older drum brake units to provide better stops while retaining the old world look. These choices will be far more limited as modern technology has taught us better ways to slow machinery and the drum brake system seldom adds up to adequate stopping power.

Each of these decisions and processes will be discussed at greater length later in this book but this should give you a basic thought plan to arrange for the adaptations you'll choose to make later.

BUILDING A RACING CAFÉ MACHINE

There are going to be some who have the desire and need to build their Café Racer to be just that, a racer. In today's world there are several sanctioned bodies that are organized to facili-

Although better known for their twin-cylinder models the Ducati line was powered by single-cylinder models in the early days of their lineage.

One of the better known Hondas, powered by their venerable inline-four is often converted to Café Racer status and the low bars and solo saddle are evidence of the change on this copy.

tate racing events at regional tracks. The AHRMA is one of the biggest and best organized and can guide you to what machines are best suited for each level of racing. Those parameters will help you to more carefully make the needed decisions for buying and building a pure race machine.

If racing will be the only application for your Café Racer then many of the previous rules can be discarded. Sound levels, lighting and related issues are not pertinent when taking to the track and will open up a brand new set of avenues for you to pursue. Obviously this wide open cornucopia will also bring never before experienced levels of expense as racing gear tends to be purpose built and leaves no stones unturned. This turning of stones can also be called R&D which costs money to process. The end result is nearly always a product that is far superior to what can be bought for the street riding market and be well worth the added costs. When walking through the pits at Road America in Wisconsin I am always stunned

by the amazing display of hardware being put to use on the track. Even some of the privateer teams are using exotic chassis and running gear to conquer the circuit. The engineering prowess that's available today can be seen at every level in life even at the track.

A true race machine will be built using the best chassis available and be powered by an engine that is created to ring every horsepower it can from the given displacement. Racing rules will dictate what levels of output and displacement can be attained and will need to be adhered to strictly if you plan on keeping any trophies you bring home. Once you've selected the class of racing you hope to participate in you can better decide what motorcycle and alterations can be made and at what cost. As the old saying goes "to make a small fortune in racing, start with a large one…"

Nearly every segment of the vintage racing has a different set of guidelines to allow riders of all skill levels and equipment a chance to participate.

Built using a 2010 Triumph Bonneville T100 this Café Racer, property of Amy Mellinger, has the look of the vintage machines with the dependability of the new. After ceasing production in 1983 the original factory was rebuilt a few years later and the brand was reborn fitted with modern engines and vastly improved chassis. The Triumph name was first seen in 1883 so their history has been one of longest in history.

By reviewing the options and choosing the class of racing that best suits your skills and hardware you can enjoy more of the action and still stay safe and within your budget. Having taken the first step towards running your Cafe Racer on the track the next step is to locate the machine that will serve you well while not breaking the bank.

An important decision to make before delving too deeply into the world of racing is to ensure your plans coincide with the hardware you can find. I'm sure anyone who plans on starting their career in racing would love to find a bargain priced ex-world superbike just collecting dust but the odds of that are slim. Failing that option you'll need to determine what your chosen class of racing will be before heading out to find the equipment you need to compete at the level you have selected and are qualified for.

Once again an entire book can be written on building a race machine but all we suggest is that you follow the rules set out by the governing bodies, choose gear that will work for you and have fun. Whether you intend on racing or riding on the street these thoughts still apply so use your head before taking matters to action.

Drawing breath through a pair of K&N pods enhances performance and also harkens back to the early days of the Café Racer scene.

A set of Norman Hyde handlebars make the rider's posture more aggressive and add to the steering response due to the closer proximity to the front forks.

Chapter Three

Choosing

Choosing A Motorcycle to Create Your Café Racer

Odds are, if you have decided to buy or build a Café Racer for your own use it isn't your first foray into the world of motorcycling. Almost every person I've spoken to about the craft has been a long time rider with experience on a variety of different machines. Some will choose a cycle they are familiar with or already own to begin the project. Other more adventurous types will start from scratch, searching for the perfect donor bike then working out the plans for the conversion.

A primary concern when making any motorcycle purchase is your physical size and how

An obvious choice to begin your Café Racer project might be one the classics from the country where the trend was born. The Triumph Bonneville is an iconic machine that remains a favorite of collectors and riders of all stripes. The design lends itself well to a Café Racer conversion and a large amount of parts can be found to make the change. Owner: The Dobbs Collection

you plan on riding the machine. If you are shorter in stature or over 6 feet tall, the size of the motorcycle you ride should be tailored to best suit your own personal dimensions. Smaller riders should consider how well their feet will reach the pavement when they bring their ride to a halt. Being able to rest at least one foot on the ground solidly is a safer way to choose a cycle. The weight also plays a role as you will at one point or another need to move the cycle while not seated on it. Parking or moving around in your garage both require your ability to manage the size and weight of the motorcycle without a dangerous level of effort. If and when you accidentally drop your motorcycle onto its side, be sure you are able to lift it upright even if you are alone.

If all you plan on doing is some weekend jaunts to local haunts, your focus on comfort will take a backseat to performance and even appearance. Clip-on handlebars look perfect on a Café Racer but riding long distance on a cycle with them in place causes more discomfort than most adults can stand. You can try to fake it and claim it doesn't bother you, and as long as the same people aren't around in the morning when you groan getting out of bed you are fine. Plans to ride longer distances will require a more comfortable saddle which will also alter your riding posture. Modifying or select-

Deciding to stay on a more classic path for your Café Racer, choosing a Triumph is never a bad choice. Early examples of the Trophy's were powered by a 500cc twin and later units carried 650cc in the frame. Deemed a terrific all-around machine in stock trim it also makes a nice starting point for your Café Racer conversion. Owner: Ken Rottman

Another terrific starting point for a Café Racer is the Honda CB750 and there are a huge amount of parts being sold for these big machines. Owner: Ray Landy

The triples from Kawasaki provide an exciting platform from which to create your Café Racer as long as you are familiar and comfortable with their quirky powerband. Owner: Keith Campbell

A great beginning for a more traditional Café Racer is the 350 models from Honda, whether low-pipe or high. They are dependable, easy to maintain and many parts can be had without too much effort.

If the 500cc Mach II from Kawasaki isn't enough of a challenge the 750cc Mach IV might be up your alley, though it's classic status may get you some odd looks from the purists. Owner: K. Campbell

ing a different fuel tank makes a strong statement but can really mess with your options when it comes to riding any distance. Some of the really cool aftermarket tanks are really limited in how much fuel they can carry so keep that in mind when selecting a new design.

CAFÉ RACERS ALREADY ON THE STREET

One of the goals of this book will be to illustrate the varying ways to build a Café Racer and how others have already accomplished the task. By showing different completed models from nearly all walks of the motorcycle arena our hope is to inspire you to choose a direction and begin gathering the necessary bits and pieces you'll need for the project. Obviously your budget will dictate which direction is best and if you can hire trained people to do your work or if you'll take the wrenches into your own hands to make the alterations. The early nature of Café Racers was one of simplicity with owners doing any work they desired and could find parts for. Today's café market is full of available catalog parts, making your choices more numerous but easier to attain.

The old world way forced you to attend swap meets and salvage yards to locate the component you sought for your creation. For some that type of search is still rewarding and makes for an enjoyable way to spend a day. The Source Guide at the end of this book provides you with a long list of vendors catering to the Café market and all will make your life easier when assembling a machine of your own.

FACTORY CAFÉ RACERS

Manufacturers have offered "factory" café racers for decades with varying levels of success. The Italian companies were some of the earliest to venture down that path and a few have become cherished treasures among collectors. As early as 1920, Demm was producing motorcycles in Italy. In 1971 they built the Sport 50 which came with café style bars, bodywork and seat. Another fabled Italian firm is Moto Morini with roots going back to 1937. For 1962 they produced a 49cc machine named the Corsarino that carried a set of lowered bars and racy bodywork. The early '70s saw a number of these models coming from Ducati and their heritage lent itself well to sculpting a café style machine from the existing designs. Lucky for Ducati, performance was already blended into their DNA resulting in primarily cosmetic changes to bring one of their cycles into the Café format. By adding a front fairing and rear seat cowl they quickly converted existing models into something that appealed more to the new café riders. Ducati has earned a terrific reputation with their high-performance offerings through the years and always make a great place to start if you have a few extra dollars to spend. Another of the Italian makers to produce factory Café Racers was Moto Guzzi. Their LeMans 850III was also named for a famous race course in France and wore a tiny café fairing and touted nimble handling and better than average performance. Laverda and Bimota are a few other Italian marques that have long histories of building sport and Café motorcycles that are sold directly to the consumer. From Bavaria BMW brought us their R/90S which was fitted from the factory with a sport fairing, two-up yet Café inspired seating and the iconic Sunburst paint. Regarded as one of the longest running machines on the road despite their age, you can find them at local shows and events today looking as good as they did new.

Despite the fact that a vast majority of Café machines hailed from Europe or Japan, Harley-Davidson tried their hand at building a factory Café Racer in 1977. The XLCR was a distinctive machine based on their smaller Sportster platform. A slim tail section was matched with a bikini fairing up front. A Siamese exhaust system was finished in black as was nearly every inch of the frame and sheet metal. It was only sold for two years as mainline Harley buyers weren't big fans of the Café trend.

Factory Café machines from the Japanese manufacturers flourished in the latter part of the '70s and into the early part of the '80s. Many of these models were little more than dressed-up versions of their existing models but typically were also given performance and handling upgrades to better suit the image. Several of these models have become collectible in today's market due to their

Another traditional offering from Honda is their 350G, meant for street use only. Again, these machines are reliable and parts can be located with ease. Owner: Steve Searles

If a 3-cylinder engine better suits your needs the Trident might fill the bill. It won't be as easy to attain or maintain, but still makes a terrific platform for a Café Racer. Owner: www.BradsBikes.net

Honda's history gives us all a really vast array of machines to choose from and the 360cc models were fairly close to the earlier 350s but carried slight improvements.

Making its debut in 1973 alongside the RD60 and bigger RD350 the RD250 makes another classic choice for today's Café Racer. Their light weight, nimble handling and fun factor bring a lot to the table. Owner: David Lucas

limited sales or import in the days of their being offered. The 1979 Suzuki GS1000S, otherwise known as the Wes Cooley Replica only saw 700 copies sent to the U.S. that year making them a scarce commodity today.

The 1978 Kawasaki Z1-R was another example but saw sluggish sales when new, creating a hugely attractive model to collectors today. 1989 saw Honda release the GB500 in probably the truest form of factory Café Racer to be sold in the USA.

Most of the factory machines are best left alone as a basis for making a Café Racer of your own devices as their original intent was to fill that slot as designed. For 1979 Yamaha sold a Daytona Special version of their venerable RD400 and was named for the legendary race course in Florida. Yamaha introduced the XJ-550 Seca for 1981 and it wore a sporty Café fairing and race inspired graphics. The fabled two-stroke RD model returned for 1984 and was available dressed in the yellow and black Kenny Roberts edition paint. The bikini and small chin fairing added to the mystique of the winning rider and machine.

MOTORCYCLES THAT WOULD MAKE A GREAT CAFÉ RACER

Having made the decision to build a Café Racer today, there is a myriad of

Carrying a sporty nature in its genes the SS models from Honda are also a perfect platform to base your Café Racer on. Changes to the bodywork and controls are about all you'd need to create a great Café entry.

available machines that await your talents. Years, makes and models range from the smaller 200cc examples up to some of the larger liter sized cycles. A Café Racer tends to be based on a smaller displacement model due to their enhanced handling and nimble convenience. Lucky for us there are no hard and fast rules when building a Café Racer thus opening up a vast cornucopia of cycles waiting for your call. There are machines powered by both two and four-stroke motors with either selection delivering an entirely contrasting performance envelope. The two-stroke variants were often considered to be a "light switch" power plant. It was either off or on with very little delay in between. While providing a more spirited ride previous experience with these perky motors is highly suggested. As I recall another common nickname for the two-strokes was "widow maker". Great name for a rock band but not when applied to a machine you choose to ride for fun.

Of the many options, Yamaha's RD models rank high among fans of the Café breed. The Kawasaki triples are another popular option as they were fairly capable when they left the factory, needing only minor enhancements in the drive train department to enjoy a high adventure ride. Honda brought us the CB450 which may have had a smaller motor than some of the competitors it made for

In the same family as the 550 edition, Honda offered their bigger 750 model wearing the similar curvaceous exhaust, different graphics and a slim tail section.

Although sold right alongside the 550 and 750 versions of the other SS models the 400 has earned the biggest following. The smaller size and list of appealing features make a nice place to begin your Café Racer journey. Owner: Keith Campbell

Selling their first four-stroke machines in 1977 Suzuki also had a 550, 750 and 400cc version in the catalog and the 750 was probably the most versatile for daily riding or longer distance jaunts. A few tweaks and you're Café ready. Owner: Bill Abdou

an amazing combination of looks and handling. Nearly all of the early machines from Japan were of the two-stroke design until the latter part of the '60s and well into the '70s. Many if not all of the early machines were built around stamped steel frames which were pleasant to ride but hardly a perfect choice for someone hoping to do some aggressive riding once converted to Café status. The tubular steel frames of the later models provided a far more stable platform to build an eager Café cycle from and can be easily updated with all sorts of modern hardware available today. The long history of imported motorcycles gives you a huge display of possible machines from which to choose.

Combining the years of manufacture with the number of makers leaves you with literally 1000s of options.

All I suggest is that you do some research in advance to determine your best choice. Doing some background into available parts will also aid your process and help you avoid getting a terrific bike that has few mechanical or cosmetic options in the world.

The Honda CB200 has been converted into a modern Café Racer by more than a few owners with great results. Honda sold several variations of this model through the years including street and dual purpose versions, allowing you a greater choice when selecting hardware to assemble your Cafe machine. Honda set

This example of the CB750 Super Sport is not exactly in stock trim but a very nice copy and a great starting point for a Café Racer conversion. Owner: Route 31 Hot Rods

the stage for two-wheeled domination when they introduced their CB750 for 1969. Motivated by a massive (at the time) four-cylinder motor displaced 736cc and was fitted into a stout, tubular steel frame. It is still coveted by collectors and made for a high performance café racer then and today.

The Kawasaki four-stroke camp also provides a wide array of potential cycles for your project. The KZ200 was one of the smallest machines sold by Kawasaki but remains a very simple and easy to maintain machine today. The KZ model range saw 400, 550 and larger variants roll into view through the years. Twin and four-cylinder options still remain, allowing you to further customize your selection. Adding the GPz moniker to their sportier machines, Kawasaki upped the ante for entertaining cycles by introducing near-race bikes for the street – with plenty of Café options available as well. The 1966 W1 was sold by Kawasaki and closely mimicked a British machine in its sheet metal and twin-cylinder motor. It remained on the Kawasaki dockets for several years and was later offered in more sporty versions but never broke records for sales. 2000 saw the W650 return to the fold and once again mirrored an offering from Britain but this time with modern electronics and running gear. With very limited production runs for both cycles, neither the W-1 or W650 are commonly seen on the

A more exotic start for your Café Racer would be anything from the Moto Morini family but a small selection of parts and a keen knowledge of how to keep them running are important factors to consider. Owner: www.bradsbikes.net

Beginning with a modern machine like Triumph's T100 Bonneville makes the end result easier to reach with dealer support and entire catalogs of parts at your fingertips. Owner: Motor Cycle Center (MCC)

Taking another dip into the Italian waters we find the Moto Guzzi V7 at our avail although once again it has its limitations in aftermarket parts being offered but doesn't lack much in the performance department. Owner: Joe Bortz

market today but would both make nice starting points for a contemporary Café machines.

Suzuki also presents us with a large selection of potential Café project machines. Although not sold in the states until 1963, Suzuki was quick to catch up with the other Japanese competitors with their range of models. The earliest of the Suzuki machines worthy of a true Café conversion was probably the X-6 Hustler. As it was built, the X-6 came with a 247cc motor in a tubular frame with seating for two and terrific handling. It has earned nearly a cult following in today's collector market but many can be found in condition worthy of converting into a very useable Café Racer today. 1968 saw a larger 500/Five from Suzuki which reappeared as the Titan in 1969. The first four-stroke models from Suzuki weren't sold until 1977 but the new GS series would become an instant favorite due to their clean design and reliable inline-four motors. Seen in 400, 550 and 750cc versions it appealed to riders of all sizes and riding skills. The GS family would grow to 1000 and 1100cc variants in the coming years and were still competent machines but maybe a bit big for a typical Café Racer.

The last of the major Japanese manufacturers was Yamaha and they began selling their motorcycles in the states beginning in

Hailing from China the SYM Wolf Classic 150 is a smaller machine but still offers loads of choices at a bargain basement price. As time goes by I suspect there will be tons of parts being created for these nimble and affordable two-wheelers. Owner: Moto-Scoot

1962. The YDS-3C appeared for 1965 and was named the Big Bear Scrambler. Powered by a 250cc motor it was a diverse machine then and now.

The high-mounted exhaust pipes made it a "scrambler" but the rest of its layout was pure street. 1967 saw a bigger YR-1 Grand Prix come into view sporting a 348cc mill in its steel tube frame. The 1970 R-5 was the next generation of sporting Yamahas and was based on their racing version RD-56.

The highly capable RD series made their debut for 1973 and were first offered in 250 and 350cc variants. The RD family would soon reach epic popularity with their amazing handling and terrific fuel mileage when the gas crunch hit.

In the last few years a new range of offerings has been heading the USA from China. Much like their four-wheeled siblings they offer a great vehicle with a low cost of entry.

They lack some of the refinements of the other machinery on the streets but still provide adequate power and safety for the money. One such brand of two-wheeled craft wears a badge from SYM. Their Wolf Classic 150 carries a 150cc, four-stroke motor in its frame and can be had for an MSRP of only $2999 brand new. Although the catalog of available Café Racer parts may be slim today the growing ranks of riders and buyers will change that situation soon. SYM is only the latest

Although hardly a lightweight cycle the XS750 triple provides adequate power based on a stable platform and can be modified without too much hassle to be your first or next Café Racer.

Ducati has a long history of building race inspired machines and their 7500SS remains one of the best. Although more sport than Café, it still rings true with the theme of the Café Racers being built then and now. Owner: Keith Campbell

This beautifully done Rickman-chassis machine was built by Craig Vetter - US importer for the Rickman in the states. Photo courtesy of and copyrighted by Craig Vetter

Another liter-size machine dressed as a Café Racer was Suzuki's GS1000S - the Wes Cooley replica. A limited number of race versions were campaigned on tracks across the USA. Owner: Keith Campbell

Even Harley-Davidson through their hat into the Café Racer ring with the 1977 XLCR complete with bikini fairing, tail section and sleek saddle. Owner: Joe Bortz

With a 400cc motor in its frame and race inspired bodywork, the Daytona Special edition of the Yamaha RD400 is a coveted machine in today's market for good reason. Owner: Paul Frisch

Kawasaki used their KZ1000 to build their own Café Racer in 1978, the Z1-R. Probably too big to be a true Café Racer it still looks the part and is a confident performer. Owner: David Freeman

A one year only model from Yamaha was the Seca 500 that came equipped with the Café fairing and racy stripes. Again, not a true Café Racer but doing what it could to fit the mold. Owner: Barbara Pugh

offering from China but joins a growing list of competent machines from that faraway land.

Turning our attentions back to the early days of the Café racers we now sort through a wide array of British and Italian models to choose from. As a rule none of these machines will come as cheaply as one of their Japanese counterparts but will probably result in a far more accurate Café Racer when completed.

With the Café trend beginning in England, British marques are still the truest form of cycle to choose for conversion and even narrowing your choices to this sliver of the overall market you'll be inundated with options. Triumph, Norton, BSA, Ariel and Royal Enfield are but a few of the

Honda's attempt at building a factory Café Racer really struck a chord with buyers and its design and execution was a true nod to the early days of the trend. Owner: Dennis French

MotoGuzzi has a long history of creating race bred street machines - the LeMans was aptly named. The compact fairing and sparse saddle add to the Café Racer blend without crossing over. Owner: Joe Bortz

Dunstall produced frames that could be fitted with an engine to build a Café Racer. The Dunstall Norton combo was very popular and looks great decades later. Owner: The Dobbs Collection

Yet another country heard from in the factory Café Racer is Bavaria with their BMW R/90S. Delivered to the dealer wearing the bikini fairing and sporty saddle the R/90S is another timeless classic.

brands representing England. Engines using single, twin or three-cylinder designs can be found along with a variety of chassis and suspension options. While some brands have drawn a higher interest level from collectors through the years some other brands have not. Finding exhaust and major components for an older Triumph will be far easier than seeking one for an Ariel. Among the Triumph name plates, the Bonneville, T100, Speed Twin and Trident are some of the more available choices. The Thunderbird would make another candidate but at the risk of annoying the purists.

A few more names can be found as well but messing with an original Brough Superior or Vincent might land you in hot water with the purists. They are always a choice but as mentioned earlier parts for these rare breeds are not common or available through modern catalogs. A few of the storied marques have returned to modern day production, Triumph and Royal Enfield are two of the biggest names. There is no rule saying you are forced to start with an old machine for your Café creation and choosing a motorcycle that was built in the last decade can save you worlds of hurt when it comes to maintenance and upgrading your parts. A warranty is nice too but may be voided when making alterations to certain segments of the cycle. Be sure to check with the manufacturer before beginning to slice and dice a warranted machine.

From the country of Italy we also find a vast selection of machines from which to choose. Ducati, MV Agusta, Moto Guzzi and Laverda are probably the premier class and will more than likely make for an expensive starting point. The list of available components for these critters will also be fairly limiting unless you are adept at trolling through swap meets or using the internet as a source to search required bits and pieces.

By choosing a Rickman frame then adding the motor designed to fit the chassis you had an almost instant Café Racer. Craig Vetter was an importer for the Rickman products in the '70s and of course is well known for his Windjammer fairings of the period too. Image courtesy of and copyrighted by Craig Vetter

Ducati remains in production today and again will provide you with a contemporary machine to build your Café Racer but cost and warranty issues need to be addressed before work begins in earnest. There is always a group of enthusiast that would argue that a modern Ducati needs no alterations to be better but when building a Café Racer you are seeking a unique ride, not trying to re-invent the wheel. Adding your personal touches to make a cycle your own is a great way to join in the fun while rising above the more common offerings being ridden today.

Depending on how radical you plan on going with your Café creation, some models off the beaten path will also serve you well in your quest. Sears, Allstate, Bridgestone and other alternate brands have been seen wearing Clubman style handlebars and perhaps a small bikini fairing to better fit into the Café mold. While their performance will lag behind some of the other offerings they may suit your individual needs to a "T". There are really no wrong answers when building a Café racer so let your own tastes and budget guide you through the process. Almost anyone involved in this hobby will be happy to assist you in your efforts to locate, build or modify a motorcycle to meet your own Café Racer needs.

The brochure for the Rickman products was a slick piece of work and told the buyer of all the benefits of using a Rickman frame for a successful machine. Photo courtesy of and copyrighted by Craig Vetter

Illustrating the Rickman design Sans motor gave the buyer the true nature of what was included when purchasing the Rickman frame and fairings. Photo courtesy of and copyrighted by Craig Vetter

Chapter Four

Chassis Mods

Café Racer Chassis Modifications

Once you've ridden a motorcycle for a while, odds are you'll want to up the ante in the performance department. For anyone who plans on spending time on a race track upgrades to the chassis and suspension should be first on your list. Certain aspects of these modifications can be made by bolting on some new shocks a change easily achieved by even the amateur mechanic. Of course buying the correct shocks that are tuned to your specific machine is key but the physical act of changing them is fairly straightforward. When changing the factory shocks to something more

Circle K Kustoms had to make several dramatic changes to the RD350 chassis to be able to accept the single shock at the rear. The pivot point was moved and a set of steel bars were created and welded to the frame to allow for the more exotic suspension.

advanced you will quickly notice the altered ride of your cycle. If this alteration alone helps you become a better rider there's no need to progress further. If however you decide to do what you can to shave more time off of your lap times at the track there are several ways to go about making changes to achieve that goal.

When making any alterations for the sake of performance please keep in mind that your skills as a rider play a heavy hand in the outcome of your modifications.

The chassis of the original Bimota was altered at the rear by replacing a section of the factory tubing with a new section to accept the mono-shock rear suspension.

Anyone can spend a ton of money on new gear but as long as their skills lag behind their budget no real gain will be achieved. Assuming you have the required skills to eke more speed out of your track laps, serious changes to the chassis can have a dramatic impact on your on-track efforts. Of course serious alterations to the chassis will also be felt on the street but many of the truly drastic modifications will actually deter the comfort of your Café Racer on the street as the surface and traffic will cut deeply into your efforts. As with any alteration be sure the changes will reflect your intentions so that end result will not stray from your planned riding.

The next consideration to be taken prior to making changes to the chassis of your motorcycle is your own skills as a mechanic along with your collection of tools and machines needed to achieve the chosen changes. It's a fairly safe bet to say that most of us have

By replacing your stock sprockets and chain with an aftermarket alloy set you'll save weight and gain the flexibility of being able to alter your gear ratios with ease. Courtesy of Economy Cycle

Pound for pound, disc brakes give more stopping power and better cooling than drums. Slotted or drilled rotors help with cooling and help to dissipate water on the rotor during stopping. Unlike factory brake lines, stainless lines do not expand under hard braking and thus give a more solid feel to the pedal or lever.

The only thing a new finish of gloss black powder coat will do for your frame is make it look better and add a long lasting gleam to your machine. Courtesy Coating Specialties

the desire to be capable of making any required changes with our own gear but shortcomings in that area will soon become apparent as you delve into the field of making the desired mods to your cycle. These are the times when turning to experts in the arena of chassis upgrades is highly recommended and even more highly suggested. Nearly every segment of the country will have shops that are well trained and equipped to creating a far better race machine so do some research to find the team that best suits your needs and pocket book. Quality in this aspect of the change is crucial and a shop that promises to do the job cheaply will more than likely make you regret the choice to save some money when creating a pure-bred race machine.

Living where I do I am lucky to have a business named Framecrafters within my grasp, at least when it comes to distance from my home. Operated by Randy and Karsten Illg, you will find two people who are not only highly skilled at their craft but Karsten turns more than a few laps himself on race tracks around the country with a great record of success. Randy is the lead shop master and his background and experience in all aspects of motorcycle chassis art is legendary. Although he is largely self-taught his range of skills began at the tender age of 10.

His neighbor had a lawn mower that refused to

start and Randy asked if he could take it home to get it going. After disassembling the motor he found the error, corrected it and had a fine running mower to bring back to the surprised owner.

His ability to grasp new challenges, learn what needs to be done and then producing the desired modifications makes him a stand-out among many others in his field. He would turn his attentions to his own motorcycles in the latter part of the '80s and grew his activities into Framecrafters in the late years of the 1990s.

Since the days he first began turning his focus to two-wheeled creations many innovations have been born of his creativity and handiwork. The latest that has sprung from his fertile mind is a triple-tree that can have its offset changed by 10mm to fine tune the handling of your machine to meet with your own riding style and preference. Randy gives most of the credit for the design of the triple tree as well as the machining to Kevin Heezen of Designs by Kevin. Adding offset reduces the trail of the chassis resulting in a quicker turning cycle. Reducing offset gives you a motorcycle that doesn't turn as sharply and better suits riders with less experience at speed.

Another bright star in his universe is the bi-metallic chassis. By melding the traits of 4130 chrome-moly tubing and 6061 billet cross-members he achieves a complete race bike that weighs a scant 200 pounds before adding fuel. Regardless of the type of racing you plan to do weight is the chief enemy of victory and eliminating it while retaining rigidity is king. The bi-metallic chassis will happily accept any four-stroke, single-cylinder motocross power plant and his prototype is fitted with a YZ250F mill. In contrast to the high-tech nature and super lightweight of this design, the cost of entry is lower than you would expect. A reasonable price point is one of Randy's goals for his latest design as the economy continues to be challenging to many wanting to begin or further their racing efforts.

In addition to his adjustable triple-tree and bi-metallic chassis Framecrafters is capable of every challenge you present as long as the desired changes don't bring dangerous aspects of the alterations to your cycle. While Randy and Karsten

Another upgrade you can make to the appearance of your Café Racer is to use a triple finish on the wheels. This example shows us the polished and pinstriped lip with powder coated spokes and polished rotor. Courtesy Coating Specialties

Once the brake assembly had been taken apart we find a bad section of corrosion on the brake piston. You may be able to correct this issue on some examples but in this case replacement is the recommended change.

With this frame bound for the race track, Framecrafters modified the upper tubes of the chassis to allow for easy removal of the cylinder head in the event of trouble.

One of their greatest creations to date is the bi-metal chassis from Framecrafters. Using a combination of alloy metals the complete cycle before fuel weighs only 200 pounds.

will be happy to tackle unusual and often avant-garde requests, anything that sacrifices safety for function or form will be denied. You can bring in almost any style and brand of cycle for conversion or upgrade and if required Randy can locate and acquire a cycle for you that will best suit your needs and desires. His favorite challenge is building complete race machines when possible but he realizes that the need for this is not as common as those simply wanting more performance from their existing crafts.

Altering the suspension, chassis characteristics and overall ride performance is well within the skill set of Randy and Karsten and they welcome your request to go faster and handle better. Their shop listing, along with many others can be found in the Source Guide at the end of this book.

CHASSIS ALTERATIONS AND FRAME GEOMETRY

For those of us who will keep our riding activities on the streets, there is no real need for radical alterations to the chassis of your motorcycle. Not only will any revisions alter the ride traits but certain modifications will actually reduce the quality of the handling and possibly even the safety of your craft. Careful review needs to be done before you decide to alter the chassis of your machine and talking to experts is of great value in advance of you turning a wrench.

Entire books have been created on the facts surrounding a motorcycle's chassis and the mathematic equations required to do it correctly. Often times, even a mild change in the dimensions of your factory chassis will result in a drastic change so caution must be exercised to achieve positive results from your efforts. During the heyday of the chopper era forks and suspension were altered largely for the sake of appearance with little or no regard for the handling. Most of those machines were seldom ridden any distance or at any rate of speed that would jeopardize the rider and passenger. Sadly we lost many a rider who disregarded the facts of nature and physics to build a wildly customized chopper only to crash while showcasing their talents as a creator of beautiful two-wheeled art.

The intent of the bi-metal frame is to save weight and deliver race-ready stiffness through the use of ultra-light alloys assembled using space age techniques.

REAR SHOCK CONSIDERATIONS

Most of the earlier motorcycles sold to the public were equipped with rudimentary yet effective shock absorbers at the rear end. Very little if any adjustments could be made to the standard settings and riders who attempted to make changes outside of the as-built specs found a handful of wasted steel on the workbench. By upgrading your original factory shocks at the rear to a set that can be adjusted for damping and preload will easily and safely bring a world of difference to your daily mileage. As always, consulting with those who have expertise in this segment of the market is crucial to buying the correct gear for your intended use and riding style. You will find an enor-

Replacing the typical trellis of diagonal tubes for rigidity, Framecrafters opted to use these blocks of alloy that are held in place by a NASA approved technique that reduces weight yet remains incredible strong.

Major revisions to the factory chassis allowed Framecrafters to install a single shock at the rear of this machine for the client. The mono-shock allows for easier adjustments and works well when used at the race track to adapt to changing conditions.

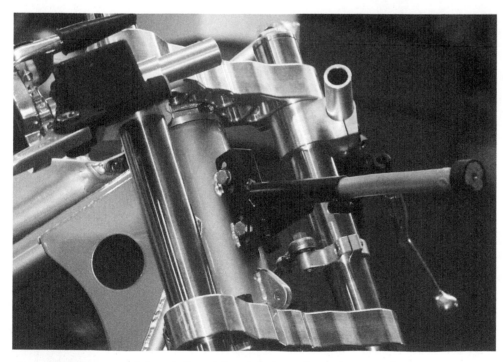

By installing a set of these adjustable triple trees from Framecrafters you can make 10mm of changes without replacing either of the trees. This allows you to custom tune the handling to suit your needs and modify it as required at a later date.

mous amount of brands and styles once you venture into the market but as with most products there are some better suited to your needs and budget. Selecting an incorrect set of rear shocks won't ruin your life but taking the time to choose the exact brand and style for your application will bring far more joy and satisfaction.

One of the easiest ways to bring a new level of handling to the table is by adding a set of gas reservoir, or "piggyback" shocks to your chassis. The design of these dampers places a smaller tube onto the back of the primary shock body and allows the gas and oil to be stored in separate chambers. This layout permits the oil to stay cooler and for the balance between the two materials to be highly adjustable. While gaining a greater amount of adaptability they do not require a vast amount of space to install. These models can be used in a two or single shock arrangement and are well suited to the racy image of your Café Racer without adding bulk or weight. Unlike some earlier systems that stored the gas in a remote canister the piggyback design allows all facets of the suspension to remain in a single unit.

By utilizing the factory mounting points for your new shocks, you will in no way alter the geometry of your chassis. Using a set that is shorter or longer than the factory plungers will have a moderate effect on your ride but won't pose any dangers. The basic math for this equation is as follows. If you install a shock that adds and inch to the height at the rear you will decrease the steering head angle by 1 degree. This modest revision will reduce trail by ¼" and result in quicker turning on a two-shock layout. Nearly the same result can be achieved by sliding the fork legs up in the triple trees by ¼". If your chassis uses a single shock at the rear there is usually enough adjustment in the shock or mounting

In order for Analog Motorcycles to change the rear suspension of the DB3 Bimota to a mono shock, the rear section of the factory frame was removed and this rectangular tube section was welded on in its place.

points to make the same revisions without replacing the OEM hardware. That is one of the benefits of a mono-shock rear suspension, the fact that you can alter the geometry with the twist of a fitting instead of creating new mounting points and reinventing the wheel with every adjustment. By choosing a stiffer spring you will also raise the ride height of the chassis.

Weight of the rider and cycle are combined and when aboard the desired sag is between 25 and 33%. All of these factors need to be considered before choosing to alter the suspension of your Café Racer so that your changes don't detract from the handling and safety of your machine. To provide shocks that will work on nearly any motorcycle layout, GAZI units are built so that you can insert different adapters into the mounting points so their shocks will fit into any pattern between 300mm and 375mm. They also offer shocks with a classic design

When open for inspection we can now see the inner fork spring as it extends out of the top of the fork tube. The spring rates can be changed by using a new spring and other revisions to fork oil viscosity will also allow you to custom tune your forks for use.

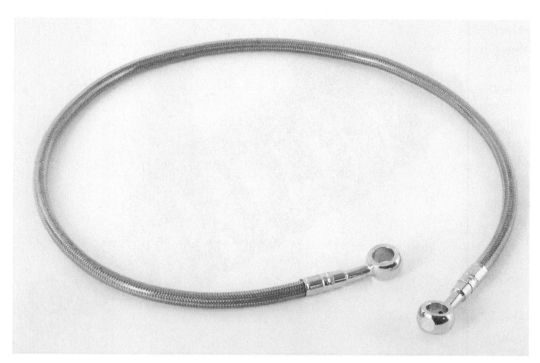

along with gas reservoir models to suit your budget and riding style. Both styles offer some adaptability but the gas reservoir units provide a wider range of adjustment and are well suited for track use.

By making changes to the rebound and compression settings on your shocks you can dial in their response to meet your riding needs. When both are adjusted correctly your rear tire will return to the pavement more quickly allowing you to regain the traction lost in the split second the chassis responded to surface irregularities.

Most modern offerings in the shock department will provide you with a vast selection of settings allowing you to choose the exact comfort and handling traits you desire on a given day. While riding solo you will want to select the setting that suit your solo mileage while taking along a passenger will require slight modifications to the options to respond to the added weight of a second person. Shocks designed more for the race-prepped cycles will more than likely use a piggyback design

Galfer is one many makers of braided stainless steel brake lines and the addition of these items will shorten your braking distance by a large margin assuming all other pieces of your braking system are up to snuff.

Another choice in GAZI's line of reservoir shocks are the Hyper Lite models. They offer many of the same features of the Hyper X at a slightly lower cost while retaining all the quality that goes into every shock from GAZI. Image courtesy Flatland Custom Cycles, Inc.

which allows the suspension to combine a higher degree of gas and springs allowing you and even greater selection of settings for comfort and handling. Many contemporary sport bikes will roll off the assembly line with this variety of shocks already installed but those cycles may be too expensive to choose as a basis for your Café alterations. Then again it is a free country and no one, or at least very few will question your logic if going that route. Progressive Suspension sells their rear shock absorbers that allow you to mix and match the pistons with springs that best suit your weight and riding style. Small adjustments are still found on the shock bodies but the choice of springs provides an improved starting point when upgrading the tail end of your Café Racer.

With both compression and rebound damping being adjustable you can tune the GAZI Hyper X shocks to meet with your exacting demands by turning two knobs. The faster you can get your tire back onto the pavement the faster you can exit a turn or accelerate down a straight. Image courtesy of: Flatland Custom Cycles, Inc.

Another function of the rear end will be to deliver the provided horsepower to the ground and by changing your sprockets and drive chain you can easily save some weight and add more convenient gear ratio changes to the game. Sold in alloys and often seen in anodized finished this will cut a few pounds off of the factory weight, provide easier swaps when needed and brings new flash to the drive train.

FRONT FORK CONSIDERATIONS

Obviously both ends of your cycle will be fitted with some form of suspension unless you've selected a very early brand and model for your Café Racer. Alterations to the front forks on a majority of available machines can be achieved but greater care

When building their Café Racer to showcase their line of products, GAZI chose to widen the swingarm to allow a bigger rear tire then bolted a pair of their own shocks in place. Image courtesy of: Flatland Custom Cycles, Inc.

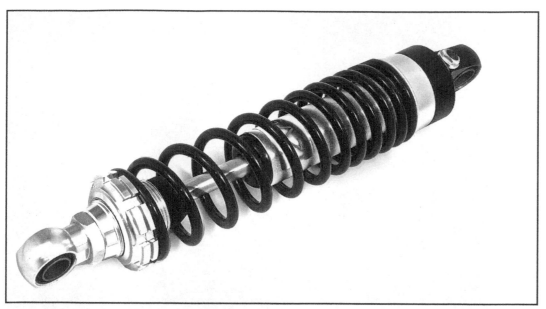

The Sport X from GAZI falls between the Classic and Hyper X models providing a high degree of adjustability. With the Sport X you get rebound and preload adjustments along with ride height modifications too. Using 6061 T6 alloy for their construction you can be assured of quality performance for years to come. Image courtesy of: Flatland Custom Cycles, Inc.

must be exercised before you choose to disassemble your forks and make any revisions.

The two easiest changes that can be made will be to the fork springs and weight or viscosity of the oil encased within the fork tubes. The stiffness of the springs installed can be changed to alter the characteristics for a personalized result. You will find fewer choices on the market when seeking springs for use in your forks and as always, careful consideration and research needs to be done in advance of your changes. Once your homework is complete and you are ready to modify the forks the process of removing and reinstalling them is fairly straightforward. Progressive is among the many manufacturers who can sell you a fresh set of front fork springs and an expert in the field can guide you to the proper choice for your riding situation.

Great care must be taken when removing your forks from the triple trees to ensure that the bearings do not get harmed or altered in any way. Older steering head bearings will probably be due to be changed and the results of installing a fresh set will sharpen up your steering without much effort. If you do

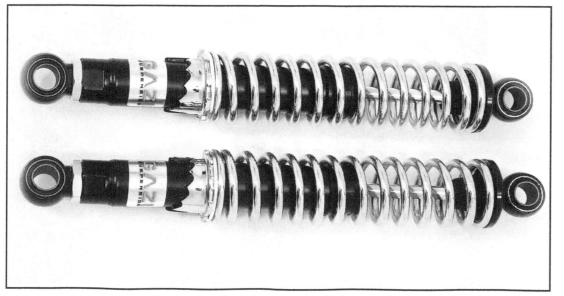

Although they lack the adjustability of their Hyper X models the GAZI Sport Classic delivers plenty of comfort with some degree of adjustment being offered at a lower price. Image courtesy of: Flatland Custom Cycles, Inc.

choose to replace the bearings in the head great care must be taken to retain the factory dimensions and settings before reattaching the fork legs.

Front fork cartridge kits will provide you with the majority of hardware required to exchange your stock components for those that will deliver better handling and more than likely provide some adjustability.

Another method of correcting the front end of your cycle would be to replace the fork assembly entirely. This can entail exchanging the fork legs for those of a more modern style or even including the triple-trees as a part of the revision. By increasing the diameter of each fork leg you'll gain increased stiffness and enhanced steering. When making that change you'll have to make sure the bigger fork leg tubes will fit into the existing triple-trees or they too will need to be swapped out. Buying the fork legs and triple-trees as a complete assembly will save you some of the dread but once again you need to be sure that the entire unit will be compatible with your chassis. Replacing the forks and all the related hardware won't be as inexpensive as changing some of the parts but the end result will be vastly improved ride and handling.

There are several sources capable of selling you a complete assembly or just the components you decide to alter so take some time exploring the options before making withdrawals from

One way to combat brake rotor warping due to heat is to use a floating rotor versus the solid steel we see on most machines. With the disc being comprised of 2 pieces the heat from the braking surface does not translate to the inner section thus keeping heat from destroying the flat metal required for safe stopping.

ISR offers a complete range of components for modern motorcycle use including these control lever assemblies that integrate a master cylinder for the brakes.

If you plan on upgrading the brake assemblies yourself be sure to carefully arrange all of the parts as they come off the cycle so you can inspect and replace without leaving anything behind.

your savings account.

The use of upside-down forks is another choice but the cost and fitment issues may cause some setbacks in that option. By design the upper fork tubes are the larger diameter of the set thus adding stiffness to the assembly. Typical fork legs have the smaller diameter tubes comprising the bulk of the assembly while the upside-down versions reverse that train of thought by having 2/3 of the fork unit being made of the stouter tubes on top. Sport bikes and racing bikes have included this design for years with great success.

As mentioned the cost of technical aspects of this option my preclude you from adding it to your plans but as always measure twice, cut once.

Adding a steering damper to the front forks will greatly smooth out feedback while turning and provide an improved feel. Bolting to the top triple tree and somewhere on the frame the simple unit is little more than a fancy door closer on the screen door at home. It can also be adjusted to the resistance level that best suits your riding style. It will obviously slow down steering response while parking but as in most devices of this sort the difference at slow speed is hardly noticeable.

If your machine has a fair amount of miles or still feels "sloppy" in the steering department you might consider changing your steering head bearings

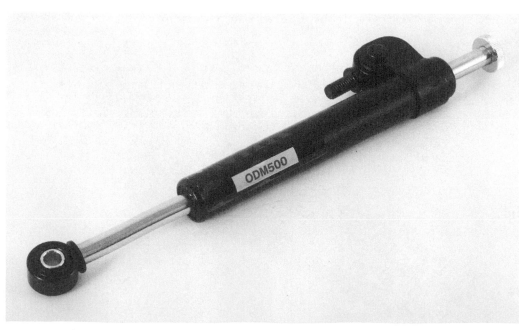

Installing a steering damper onto your Café Racer is relatively easy and will help to smooth out the corners especially when the road surface gets rough. Courtesy of Economy Cycle

46

and seals. They are usually sold in a kit to provide all of the components necessary to change every required component. Both of the wheels bearings can stand a change from time to time along with the swingarm bushings so make sure to check all of these areas when upgrading your Café Racer to provide component hardware at every point of the chassis.

STEERING GEOMETRY

As long as you plan on maintaining the factory issued steering head and its original settings no changes will be made to the geometry of the chassis. The mathematics required to safely alter the angle of your chassis' steering head is rather complex and best left to those with the expertise in doing so.

A minor alteration of a single millimeter in this angle will result in a changed handling whether you desired it or not. As we mentioned earlier there are a few makers of steering heads that allow for adjustments to be made to meet with your precise riding style. Any modifications to the angle of your front forks will result in an altered handling trait. Additional offset to the angle will provide less trail and deliver quicker, more precise handling. Less offset will give you a machine that handles more deliberately and may be a better choice for your riding plans and demands.

Making changes to the chassis that will affect the geometry of the design must be taken under careful consideration before moving ahead with the operation.

Researching the math behind this formula will tell

PartsPlusSwingarmBush Taking care to make sure the bushings and bearings on your chassis are up to date is a major step in delivering all the performance you seek from the rest of the components. The bushings that hold your swingarm in place are critical in allowing your suspension to function properly and to providing smooth motion. Courtesy of Economy Cycle

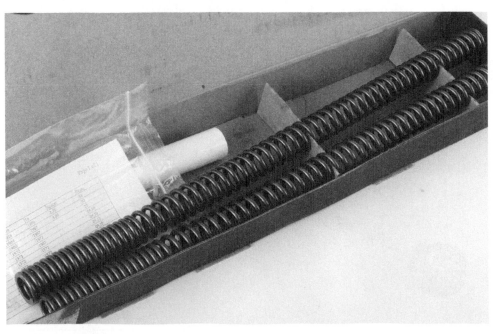

Progressive offers a wide line of products for improved suspension including springs to be used in the front forks to enhance handling and comfort. Courtesy of Economy Cycle

you whether or not you have the skills to attempt such an alteration or whether it is best left as it is or turned over to a shop that has the necessary tools and experience in this field. These changes are often seen on popular television shows but you must keep in mind that what's seen on TV has been modified to fit the program and time restraints. The most basic level of intelligence should tell you that a complete change from street to finished motorcycle cannot be achieved in 2 half-hour episodes no matter how much experience the chosen builder possesses.

"Don't try this at home" is always seen on these programs whether you

Adding some sizzle to the build, a set of Alpina tubeless rims were selected for use. Their design brings light weight and a great look to an often lackluster portion of the cycle, the wheels.

Analog Motorcycles put this Bimota DB3 through a radical makeover and in doing so swapped out the OEM brakes for a set from I.S.R.. The brakes and master cylinder are both products sold by the Swedish manufacturer.

choose to see it or not and is done for your protection to save you the grief of tackling a task that is far beyond your own skill set.

BRAKES

While going fast and handling well you'll need to consider bringing your Café Racer to a stop or at least slow down at some point. The brakes on most older cycles were adequate in their day but the science of braking has traveled light years since then. Composite materials, new shapes and floating rotor technology have all become players. Of course riding an older machine will limit your options for contemporary braking upgrades but be sure to research the market thoroughly before deciding on which direction to go. Even some older drum brakes can be revised with modern day technology although even with those improvements they will be limited by their design.

Floating rotors separate the inner portion of the brake assembly from the rotor and reduce the heat being generated from use from being transferred to the inner hub. Heat is one of the biggest enemies of a braking system and reducing it is always a benefit. Combing a new floating rotor with a multi-puck caliper adds a huge reduction in braking distance but again your machine may not be capable of carrying this modern hardware on its aging platform.

Disassembling your current brakes and checking them for wear and corrosion is one way to ensure that even OEM units are able to function when needed. Any sign of deep corrosion or pitting requires that piece to be replaced and at that point ordering an entirely new batch of hardware may be in order. You could change one piece now only to have to go through the entire process in a few months to address a different component that has failed.

One way to add some added response to your current braking system is to add a set of braided stainless steel brake lines. These lines resist the pressure of brake usage by retaining their structure even under heavy use. With sidewalls that are far sturdier than the rubber lines the improvement in stopping times should be dramatic. Using modern brake fluid can also be a benefit as long as its chemical composition doesn't interfere with your aged hardware.

By inspecting your OEM rotors for trueness and ensuring they remain flat is the easiest way to deliver competent braking from even an older bit of hardware. Once again a skilled shop with the proper equipment is best suited to check these tolerances so don't try to save a few dollars only to toss your entire project away the first time you need to stop.

Progressive also allows you to select the shock bodies and springs to custom fit their performance to your needs. Courtesy of Economy Cycle

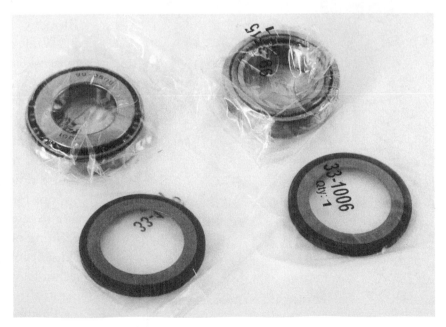

Leading the way on your chassis is the steering head and taking care to provide up to date equipment there is another method of providing years of non-stop riding fun. The bearings and seals need to be checked and replaced if any flaws are present. Courtesy of Economy Cycle

Chapter Five

Engine Mods

Café Racer Engine Modifications

As with every facet of your Café Racer conversion, modifications to the motor can be mild or extreme and you need to determine your own needs prior to beginning the process. You can make changes to the look and performance of your engine or simply clean up what you have and ride away, assuming the motor functions properly. It makes no sense to alter a motor that doesn't run as it is designed and all you'll do is throw good money after bad. If you are satisfied with the functionality of your powerplant then you can move ahead with the modifications you seek to improve

Coating Specialties can do more than apply a variety of finishes onto your Café Racer project but if desired can also polish an existing motor into a high level of gleam. By adding some chrome bits and bringing every inch to a new level of smooth the result is obvious.

the look and performance of your ride. Before delving too deeply into the purchase of any component we always suggest you do some research, talk to others who have done similar work and narrow down your search before setting out to hunt down the items you desire.

One of the easiest changes will be to bolt on a new exhaust system. The primary reason for this revision will be to enhance the breathing of your scoot which in return brings more performance. When changing from the factory exhaust system you will also have to re-jet your carburetors to provide the proper blend of air and fuel to the motor. Skipping this step will only make your machine more sluggish and deter its response to the throttle. It isn't an impossible task but does require a full set of jets to allow you to find the combination that will best suit your demands. We

Upgrading your carburetor can make a real world difference in the way your cycle runs and Mikuni has been in the business for decades. This 34mm round slide model will fit many engines but be sure it is compatible with your application prior to purchase. Courtesy of Economy Cycle

have mentioned it before but locating a local expert at this task will save you hours of frustration as you change the jets again and again before hopefully figuring out which ones work the best. A skilled shop can ask what your needs are and tailor the jetting accordingly without the fuss of going through the motions yourself.

Although the process of changing the exhaust is fairly straightforward the choices on the open market are staggering. The options will be limited dependent on the cycle you choose to fit with a new exhaust but even then you'll find a wide variety of brands, style and finishes from which to choose. If you are using an older machine to create you Café Racer you'll find a small amount of available exhaust at your fingertips. Whether your machine is powered by a single, twin, triple or four-cylinder motor will also slim down your

By joining a Yamaha manifold from the RD 350 and 400 to a K&N air filter, Economy Cycle has created another way to increase airflow into your motor.. Courtesy of Economy Cycle

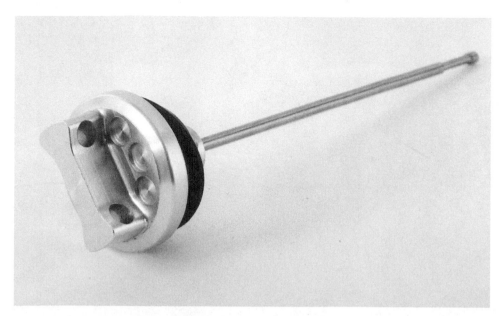

Although entirely cosmetic, adding an attractive alloy dipstick like this one brings a touch of class to what is usually a task overlooked. Courtesy of Economy Cycle

choices. If money is no object you can always find someone who is skilled at bending an exhaust to fit whatever cycle you own, but as stated this won't be an inexpensive selection.

Some of the major brands found on the market today include MAC, Vance & Hines, Bassani, Cobra, Moto-Carrera, Yoshimura and Supertrapp. Exploring the arena you'll also find Two-Brothers and Akrapovic among the contenders adding confusion to the game of finding the perfect exhaust. Another option would be to simply purchase slip-on exhausts that fit to the down tubes of your OEM system. Doing this allows you to replace rotted mufflers of the old days with a minimum of trouble, bringing new life to your creation. They can be had in a variety of styles and level of baffling within. The baffling is responsible for quieting the exiting fumes and keeping the EPA at bay. Using slip-ons will sometimes preclude you from needing to re-jet but if they deliver enough of an improvement to your motor's performance jetting will still be required for optimum results.

Finishes on most aftermarket exhaust are available in chrome

Sold by Clubman Racing Accessories this kit (part no. F304W) allows you to use a single AMAL carb in place of your factory unit to improve performance. Image courtesy of Clubman Racing Accessories

or black. If those two options aren't enough then you can always have the pipes recoated with high-temperature ceramic coating, which can be applied in a variety of finishes. These finishes add luster to an older system or bring a new level of uniqueness to your current build. Taking this path can even save you from replacing your old system at all by simply refreshing the appearance. Another method of changing the look of your exhaust would be application of heat wrap. This age old process adds a new feel to your machine while adding to the efficiency of the motor and protecting skin from being burned upon contact. Kits to achieve this effect can be found all over, and will not require much effort on your part to secure the product. Application is also not an enormous task and done properly brings a racy look to your Café Racer.

Wanting to create a two-tone theme that wasn't too extreme, Analog Motorcycles chose to have painted parts and powder coated sections live in close proximity for added depth and detail to the build.

While the exhaust is responsible for letting your engine exhale you can boost the way it inhales as well. The factory airbox is designed to answer government regulations and ensuring your carbs get the proper amount of oxygen to function as designed. While doing an admirable job at those tasks the look of the OEM box is seldom appealing and does hinder performance by choking some of the airflow. One way to improve this situation is by replacing the factory air cleaning element with an aftermarket piece that fits

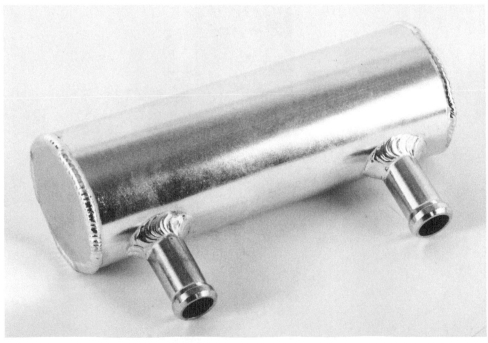

The purpose of this simple device is to smooth out the pulses typically experienced when riding a cycle powered by a two-stroke motor. It weighs almost nothing and is fairly easy to install. Courtesy of Economy Cycle

Improvements can be made to any piston by adding a thermal barrier coating to the top surface and a dry film lubricant to the sides. These coatings are designed specifically to enhance performance and longevity of the internals on a motor. Courtesy of Coating Specialties

Allowing for undisturbed flow of fuel to your motor, Pingel petcocks are well known for their products which are designed to fit nearly every application. Courtesy of Economy Cycle

If you want to boost the level of spark without replacing the entire ignition system using a mini coil from Dyna is the first step in delivering hotter spark to your cylinders. Courtesy of Economy Cycle

the same space exactly. Items of this nature are sold by K&N and UNI along with several others. These filters will keep dirt and debris out of your motor while providing enhanced breathing. Options for this dilemma can be addressed by installing a set of clamp-on air filters or "pods" as they are sometimes called. Each of these pods has its own air filter element to keep harmful dirt from getting into your motor while enhancing the amount of air flowing in. The application of the pods will also require the carbs to be re-jetted so we'd suggest you change the exhaust and airbox first before turning to the experts to re-jet. One drawback to these open pods is if you get stuck riding in the rain. Instead of the motor drawing breath through an enclosed airbox the pods draw in not only air but water, thus reducing performance immensely. Having experienced this first hand on more than one occasion I can attest to the unpleasant response the rain can have on a previously

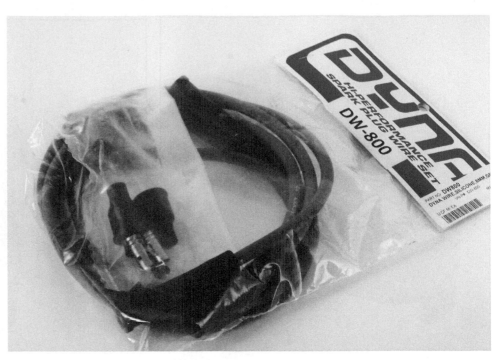

Another method of providing added spark to your motor is the installation of improved spark wires. This set from Dyna is a snap to install and works great. Courtesy of Economy Cycle

sunny day ride. There also foam variants of the pods that provide the same results while posing the same rainy day issues. The foam used on these items can usually be had in different hues allowing you to color-key them to your cycle's theme. For an even more intense look you can opt to use velocity stacks on each carburetor. These gently fluted tubes are often fitted with screen filters on their face to keep big chunks of dirt out although dust and smaller particulates will still be pulled in. Most often made from aluminum or a light weight alloy they can also be finished in a variety of plating and coatings to bring a nice level of detail to that aspect of the motor. Just like the pods in foam or screen format your carbs will need to be jetted to work properly when breathing through velocity stacks.

If you ride a two-stroke machine you are well aware of the dead spots between the power strokes. Maybe insignificant when on the

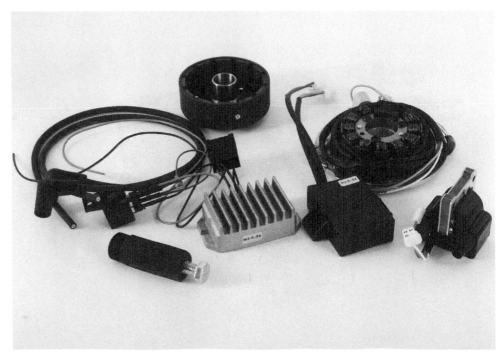

By implementing an entire electronic ignition system you will get increased spark and all of the benefits related to that improvement. It takes some time to install but most will appreciate the changes instantly. Courtesy of Economy Cycle

First seen in the early days of the hot rod, heat wrap on the exhaust improves thermal efficiency and protects flesh from being burned on contact. It brings an old school look to a modern day Café Racer.

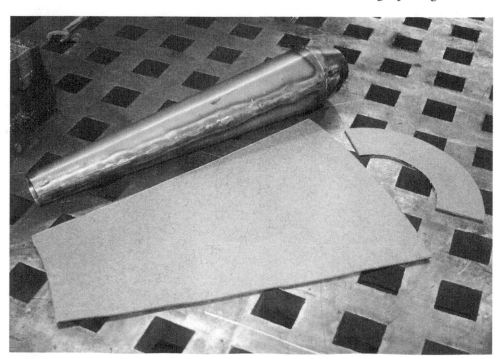

Framecrafters can not only build you a Café Racer chassis but are also capable of forming exhaust mufflers from scratch. These cardboard templates will be used to trace the shapes onto sheet metal before cutting, forming and welding into its final form.

street but when hitting the track there is a way of smoothing out the pulses by adding a Boost Bottle. This small cylindrical device simply stores a small amount of energy between pulses and provides a smoother transition to the next.

Alterations or replacing the intake manifold is another path that can be taken but your options will be really limited in this direction, even with a modern machine to start with. Riders of the classic Yamaha RD models will find a variety of items matching this description as the RDs have been used on the track for decades and racers are always seeking new ways to add power to their machines.

You can enhance the air flow by having the heads ported which is simply the process of cleaning up roughness and other flaws caused during the casting process. Race machines often employ ported heads in their efforts but once again a skilled and experienced hand will provide better results with less irritation. An unblemished surface allows the incoming air to flow freely without tumbling around when altered by small disturbances.

Regardless of what changes you make to the inflow or outflow of air, the carburetors are responsible for providing the correct mix of air and fuel to the cylinder. Fitting a proper set of carbs will be based on the size and type of motor you have and what improvements you seek. Your handiness with a set of tools will also play a part as adding aftermarket carbs requires a careful dialing in to get them to perform to their maximum potential. The basic design of a carburetor is fairly universal although the methods of achieving the same goals can be diverse. The size of the intake on a carburetor ranges from 24mm to 42mm in diameter. The correct size must be carefully determined before you clamp on a new set and expect miracles. Too

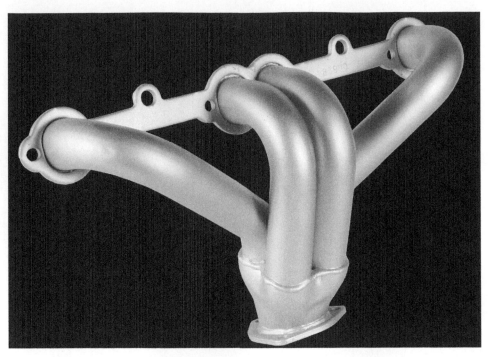

Bringing a new luster to your tired exhaust or adding a fresh level of clean to your new parts, Coating Specialties applies this high temperature ceramic coating to any part that will endure extreme temps, like an exhaust or other engine part.

small or too large can both be detrimental to the performance of the engine. Another element of their design is whether they are flat-slide or round-slide. Each of these designs brings new choices to the table and can make a huge difference in the outcome of your modifications. As a general rule of thumb flat-slide carbs work best on two-stroke motors leaving the four-stroke duties to the round-slide. Another general rule tells us that the flat-slide editions work best at higher RPMs and suffer at low or mid-range speeds. The reason we often see flat-slide carbs on race bikes is because all they use is the upper end of the rev range once they leave the pit lane. Using flat-slide carbs will also require a much higher degree of tuning to deliver the performance on tap. Tuning them demands a high level of skill and patience as they require delicate tweaking to achieve the output you seek. Some who are experienced in both brands of carburetion simply state that with enough tun-

Coating Specialties offers a range of five different colors to high heat ceramic customer allowing them to choose the finish that best suits their needs while keeping style a part of the plan.

By adding an external oil cooler to the blend you can extend the life of your motor due to the increased cooling power delivered by the air flowing through the blades of the unit. Mounting brackets and fittings for the oil lines will need to be created unless your spare parts bin already contains them.

As we already know the RD series from Yamaha enjoys a bounty of parts that can boost performance and these high performance manifolds are among the rest. Courtesy of Economy Cycle

ing, jetting and skill the right person can get any setup to run as planned.

Having decided between flat and round-slide design you will once again face a myriad of brand names in the field. Mikuni, Dell'Orto, Keihin, S&S are among the better known with Caltric and Yost joining the ranks. Mikuni and Keihin have been used on Japanese cycles from the factory for decades and provide the user with a great number of parts to maintain and correct any troubles that can pop-up later in life. Typically you'll find the S&S models best suited for use on Harley-Davidson motors as they have been producing carbs for that market for years.

Assuming you've sorted out the issues with carburetion, intake and exhaust there's one more factor to be considered before you can ride away to enjoy your new cycle. A good spark is required to light off the air and fuel mix no matter how it's delivered to the manifold. At the heart of this family will be the ignition system that provides the energy needed to fire the spark plugs to life.

Most early designs were of a mechanical design that worked fairly well considering the state of the union. Modern enhancements allow you to install an electronic ignition system which delivers a more consistent and dependable spark while also allowing

for easier adjustment.

A majority of these electronic options are contained in a small box that can be easily concealed beneath the bodywork no matter how scant it may be. Wiring them into an older setup is also fairly simple and will provide tremendous results as long as directions are followed and no shortcuts are taken.

Delivering the energy to the spark plugs is the duty of the spark wires and they too can be upgraded to modern specs without a lot of difficulty. The latest wires tend to be of larger diameter than the stock units and are composed of silicone material that provides a higher level of protection against wetness. Their heavier gauge walls also permit you to install them with less fear of them shorting out when coming in contact with the metal frame and other components on the chassis.

Any portion of your cycle's motor that doesn't require a high-temp finish can be dressed up with a wide range of powder coat finishes and colors. Yellow Ribbon is the name of this hue and will look great for years to come. Courtesy of Coating Specialties

One of the final factors in this equation is the spark plug itself. Using a design that was crafted over 100 years ago the latest spark plugs embody new materials in their tips and can deliver a hotter spark with less energy. Choosing and installing the proper spark plugs is another crucial step in arriving at peak performance. The level of spark delivered can be determined by the designation printed on each plug. Selecting plugs that are too hot or not hot enough will also hamper output so choosing the proper plug for your application is crucial.

Of course getting the fuel from

Bringing a racy look to your Cafe Racer would be the use of velocity stacks. They use a screen on the front to filter out big bits of debris but allow smaller amounts to pass through. Not a wise choice for life in the desert or in badly fouled air.

the tank to your carbs is also crucial and in many cases the ancient petcock assigned to the task is well beyond its youth. Changing out the OEM unit with a modern unit from Pingel will ensure proper delivery of the precious fuel to where it's needed. Of course an inline fuel filter will also assist in keeping stray dirt out of your carbs and they can be found in plastic or metal some in attractive anodized finishes to bring style to your lowly fuel lines.

A more aggressive agenda might find you making changes to the internal parts of the motor. In most cases this won't be attempted unless being built for track use only or to repair a damaged component. Valves, pistons and connecting rods can all be damaged if the motor is not properly lubricated or run at extreme speeds. The camshaft and even the crankshaft can be injured if operated under poor conditions

The RD and RZ machines from Yamaha have a long list of available choices when it comes to upgrading and pistons are among them with several makers offering choices such as Wossner. Courtesy of Economy Cycle

but doing that usually results in a complete destruction of the motor.

If all you seek is better power the pistons, valves and connecting rods can all be changed as long as careful consideration is given to proper selection and complete functionality between each operation. Pistons designed to increase compression can interfere with valve operation if clearance is not checked and altered if necessary. By adding certain coatings to a piston you can increase heat resistance and friction, both of which are enemies to and engine's performance. Lighter valves can function at greater speeds due to their decreased weight bringing added performance at higher RPMs. Stiffer valve springs will ensure they avoid floating at higher speeds as well, thus eliminating another power robbing side effect.

A more aggressive cam can be installed to enhance the valve operation but it too must be selected based on the remaining components and the end results demanded. Careful timing needs to be adjusted and applied to avoid the components from coming in contact when in operation. Nothing will ruin your day faster than bending a valve or cracking a case because the internals aren't getting along.

UNI Filters makes an entire line of filtration products for the transportation field and this red foam model was chosen to keep the air clean on a CB200 from Honda.

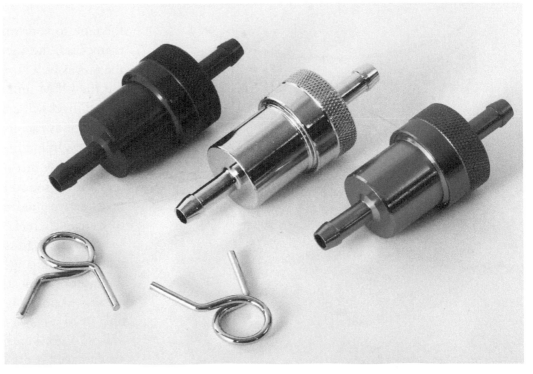

Having an inline fuel filter in place is always suggested and by using these nicely anodized versions you can bring some beauty to an otherwise mundane aspect of your café Racer. Courtesy of Economy Cycle

UNI is another choice when seeking an improvement in air cleaners whether it's for within the factory airbox or swapping the original gear for an entirely new setup. Courtesy of Economy Cycle

By replacing the stock air cleaner element within your OEM airbox you can improve breathing without any modifications. K&N offers a wide array of options when it comes to air cleaners including those meant to fit inside your factory airbox. Courtesy of Economy Cycle

Keeping your engine cool is another important feature that needs to be addressed to ensure a long life for your motor whether enhanced or not.

Most engines are equipped with all of the cooling concerns figured out but if you plan on doing any extended performance running or riding in a lot of traffic the addition of an external oil cooler may be a decision you want to make. They are typically bolted to the front down-tubes of the chassis to put them directly into the airflow. Factory radiator locations can be more discreet but still remain well within the flow of air rushing around the machine. Unless your cycle came equipped with an oil cooler when you took possession you'll need to fashion brackets to secure it as well as fittings to permit the oil to flow back into the motor after its trip through the cooler.

COSMETIC ALTERATIONS

While the previous addressed the mechanical changes that can be made to your engine, some of you may want nothing more than to dress up what works. Older motors tend to take on a faded appearance especially if they've been stored outside or under poor conditions. The cases can often be cleaned up with solvents and plenty of elbow grease as long as care is taken to choose a proper cleaning material before taking it to the precious metal of your motor. Outer cases are usually nothing more than covers for what's going on inside but they too can get dingy with the passage of time. Depending on their condition you may be able to polish out the imperfections to return them to their gleaming glory.

For light surface rust on any chrome you can moisten aluminum foil and rub it on the effected location to remove without too much effort. A bit of chrome polish after and you're good as new assuming the rust didn't pit the metal too deeply. Of course replacements can be sought in the usual places and that may be easier for you or at least bring all the covers on the motor back to a consistent finish.

Blemished covers and other surfaces can also be painted or powder coated to bring a new look to the build. As seen elsewhere in these pages, powder coating can be applied in 1000s of colors and makes for a durable and attractive finish on nearly any metal item. By combing painted and powder coated surfaces you can also create a nice contrast of textures and a subtle color palette when warranted.

The new world of billet aluminum parts has brought many new components to today's market including dip sticks used to check oil levels on your motor. A small detail perhaps, but a nice touch.

Plating can also be applied to components that are of the correct nature and can withstand the intense application process. Once plated with chrome or gold the resulting finish will remain gleaming with proper care and non-abrasive polishes.

If the twist of your throttle is simply too long, adding this throttle kit from Motion Pro will shorten the distance allowing for quicker access to all-out acceleration. Courtesy of Economy Cycle

Another method of filtering the incoming air to your motor is a set of individual pods. These attach to the opening of the carbs and keep dirt and pollutants out while letting plenty of air in.

Chapter Six

Gallery of Café Racers

In this chapter we will show you a variety of machines that were built to play in the Café Racer sandbox. As we all know by now there are many ways you can conceive and build a Café Racer and I have found many variations in my travels. Some are based and built using more traditional methods while a few have gone down the more exotic pathway. The only things restraining you from following either path is your imagination and checkbook.

The machines here are listed in no particular order although every example is worthy of being at the head of the class. We hope that by showing what has been done it might inspire you to build something that has yet to be done. I have yet to find two machines that look even remotely similar so there's no reason why you can't go out and build another that is uniquely your own. With so many parts and components available on the market today you won't have too much trouble seeking what you need and putting it to use.

The Triumph Thruxton was a new model for 2004 but had originally been sold in 1965. The new Triumph version carries an 865cc parallel–twin motor in its frame and is designed to have a sporting nature. Stan has opted for several upgrades in both appearance and performance modifications making it his perfect street machine.

2009 Triumph Thruxton

This is not Stan's first Thruxton and may not be his last. Starting a project with a terrific, modern machine takes a lot of the guesswork out of the equation and leaves you with a great end product. Leaving most of the factory body panels alone he added an Air-Tech AJS Dunstall replica fairing and Zero Gravity windscreen. A pair of Ohlins piggy back shocks at the tail end provide added control while the front forks are supported by a Super Brace. Spiegler stainless steel brake lines also bring an added measure of precision to the stopping while the British Customs Predator exhaust helps the Thruxton to breath. Rear sets from LSL and levers from Pazzo bring some machined glamour to the tidy appearance of this contemporary build.

The addition of the Ohlins piggy back rear shocks enhance ride control and comfort and look great doing so.

A Zero Gravity windscreen was added to the AJS Dunstall replica fairing for a hint of vintage on this modern day Café Racer.

65

1975 Suzuki T500M Titan
Owner: Angel Perez

Even though it's built using a vintage Japanese motorcycle, Angel's Titan has the instantly recognizable look of a classic Café Racer. Starting with the clubman bars up front to the sloping tail section out back the very spirit of the bygone days are captured. The gleaming green and white paint scheme was achieved using hours of preparation and spray cans for the finish. The 492cc motor gave Angel some trouble at first but he eventually sorted out the issues to create a strong running bike. K&N pods provide freer breathing while the factory exhaust calms the departing fumes. The solo saddle and matching tail section complete the theme and add some classic flair to a venerable Suzuki.

By using a set of true clip-on handlebars, Angel once again returns to the days of old when many riders in the Café scene were forced to use what was available unlike today's riders who have a huge array of catalog choices at their disposal.

Taking a more traditional path, Angel Perez selected a 1975 Suzuki Titan T500 for his Café Racer conversion. The two-stroke, twin-cylinder motor was a popular choice in the day and it would be two more years until Suzuki offered a four-stroke motor for motorcycle buyers. Alterations to his Titan gave it the right stance and added power that is reminiscent of the early Café Racer pioneers.

Replacing the more heavily cushioned saddle with a more austere seat and tail section tell a big portion of the Café Racer tale.

The gently curved tail section is another clue to the early days of the Café Racer and is treated to the same green and white paint as on the fuel tank. In keeping with the spirit of the first Café Racers, Angel applied the paint himself using spray cans and lots of preparation.

Leaving the original tank in its true form, the green paint with white accent stripe makes a bold statement for the minimalist design of this Café Racer.

67

1996 Bimota DB3 Mantra

Builder: Analog Motorcycles Owner: Sam Loeffler

Analog Motorcycles has five builds on the 2012 schedule and this Bimota conversion was one of the most aggressive and radical on record. The client came to Analog with some ideas for the build and then combined his concepts with Tony's input before work began. The 904cc Ducati motor remains as the powerplant but nearly every other facet of the Italian bike was altered. The rear section of the Bimota frame was removed and replaced with a freshly minted section of alloy tubing. Front forks were powder coated with no internal modifications. Brakes come via the Swedish firm of I.S.R. including the master cylinders. Tubeless rims from Alpina bring a nice accent of color to the deep gray finish on the sheet metal all of which was custom formed for this build. Exhaust tubes were also hand bent and mated to custom tips with only a minimum of sound reduction. A sleek L.E.D. tail light is discreetly mounted beneath the rear tail section and the headlight boasts its own set of L.E.D. turn signals within the front element.

Using an exotic Bimota for the basis of a Café Racer may not be a common choice but Analog Motorcycle clients want more than a common result when bringing them a project. Very few segments of the original motorcycle were left unchanged as the owner and Analog pushed the envelope at every stage of the build.

Leading the way either day or night is this modern headlight that features two sets of high intensity L.E.D.s on either side of the headlight bulb that function as turn signals.

Floating rotors, calipers and master cylinders are all products of I.S.R. a specialty manufacturer in Sweden. Their production numbers are very small but their components are amazing.

The I.S.R. master cylinder and brake lever assembly is a work of art and once adjusted works like a fine tuned instrument. The grips are treated to the same finish as found on the wheels and trim.

Perhaps seeming typical for a Café Racer, even the seat and rear tail section had to be custom made to work with the modified frame.

Honda CB200

As we know the Honda CB200 makes for a great starting platform for a Café Racer. Circle K Kustoms wanted to build something that gave a nod to the original Ace Café in London the birth-place of the Café Racer trend. The checker-board paint scheme is highlighted with Ace Café branding which gives a nice contrast to the basic black paint. A set of VW mufflers are held in place by connecting rods that also hide the weld between the shortened pipes and mufflers. In lieu of a tachometer a small skull rotates on the tach shaft when the bike is running. In order to utilize a pair of velocity stacks on the carbs two notches had to be cut into the frame's upright. To reinforce the structure a section of steel pipe was welded in to secure that section. This machine's build is also covered elsewhere in this book in greater detail.

Adding Ace Café badges to the black and white checkerboard motif tells the world their intentions right off the bat and looks great too.

As we have already witnessed, Richard Weslow knows how to build a Café Racer that's filled with creative twists. Choosing to give homage to the Ace Café in London they chose a Honda CB200 for the conversion this time around. Although far less radical than their RD350 seen in these pages the CB200 still has plenty of unique features to bring it to the forefront of the Café Racer world.

To make the pair of velocity stacks work, they had to cut half-moons out of the frame then weld in steel inserts to return the strength required - innovative techniques at work.

Nicknamed "the noodle" the length of tubing holding the tail light in place is actually a rigid length of steel tubing not a flexible section of material.

Connecting rods from a different machine help to hold the exhaust in position and also hide the welds between the exhaust tube and VW silencers.

GAZI Suspension Café Racer   Builder: GAZI Suspension

Built to be used as a rolling showcase of their suspension components, GAZI assembled this hybrid from a variety of cycles. The frame is from a 1969 Triumph Bonneville and carries a motor from a 1966 Bonneville. The rockerboxes on the motor are from a 1971 Bonneville and the front forks and brakes were borrowed from a 2006 Kawasaki ZX-6. The finished product handles as well as it looks and is a hit wherever it's displayed. GAZI makes an amazing selection of suspension parts for the motorcycle crowd which add a new level of handling and comfort when bolted on.

GAZI offers a vast selection of suspension components for use on your motorcycle and they selected a pair of their own when building a rolling display of their wares. This rear shock is accented by the slotted chain guard that helps to keep the oil from reaching the rider's leg. Image courtesy of: Grant Goldenstern

Right side shows off the high-compression 650cc Triumph parallel twin. Note the Kawasaki fork, complete with dual front discs, the one-off oil tank and the high-tech oil and brake lines.

1979 Benelli SEI & SEI 1 Owner: Enrique Martinez

Hailing from Spain, Enrique builds a wide variety of custom Benelli based Café Racers. He typically increases the displacement to 1000cc on the six-cylinder motors and then adds a range of additional upgrades. Larger valves, a more aggressive cam and a bank of 38mm carbs are the starting point and only your hunger for speed and depth of your pockets determine where it ends. Further enhancements to suspension, brakes and chassis can also be ordered and he will be happy to create the exact bike you desire, all achieved with a phone call to his shop. Replica Bimota body sections add a high degree of flair to the build and a custom paint scheme also bring a unique quality to his Benelli creations.

Coming to us all the way from Spain is this amazing Benelli EI that has been enhanced in nearly every way conceivable. Starting with the six-cylinder motor bored out to 1000cc, it now breathes through a set of 38mm flat-slide carbs. Bigger valves are moved by a more energetic cam. Note the improved brakes and the sleek bodywork, all of which brings the Café Racer theme home. The builder, Enrique Martinez can build you a Benelli to nearly any degree of insanity you desire as long your checkbook can keep up the pace. Photo courtesy of Enrique Martinez

SEI 1

Similar to the bike seen above, for this bike Enrique took the equation one step farther to create one that more closely mimics a full bore race machine. Sporting the same increased 1000cc inline-six motor and trio of 28mm carburetors, this version carries a larger fairing up front, and a solo saddle and sleek tail section at the rear. A set of blackened Magni pipes allow the exhaust a smooth passage into the atmosphere and look great while doing so. He can build you one of these machines to be used for street and track, or track-only.

1982 Yamaha Virago

The owner of the Yamaha had a vision of what he wanted the final creation to look like but did not have all the skills required for the conversion. He chose Framecrafters to make the numerous and serious changes to his '82 Virago. The fuel tank began its life on a Benelli and was highly modified to fit astride the Virago frame. The seat and tail sections were also altered to fit the large frame of the Yamaha before being fitted with a custom tail light array. The swingarm was reinforced before the slots were added to the horizontal members. Drum brakes at both ends bring an old world feel to the modern day cruiser and the new creation looks far sleeker than the original Virago ever could.

When the owner of this Virago approached Framecrafters with his ideas, they weren't sure they could see the same results. After discussing the project in greater detail Ron Bautista's thoughts made more sense and the Framecrafters team went to work. A majority of the chassis and motor were to remain stock but alterations would still be employed everywhere else. A Benelli fuel tank was modified to fit the larger Yamaha's frame as was the rear seat and tail section. Modifications to the swingarm included bolstering the strength then adding the slots for appearance sake. Dual front drum brakes may seem to be outdated but even they have been improved to haul the big Virago down from speed.

1987 H-D XLCR Replica

The official Harley-Davidson XLCRs were first seen as 1977 models and were designed to be a Café Racer version of the venerable Milwaukee brand. The 1987 adaptation we see here looks very much like the original edition but carries a newer Evolution motor in its frame rails. Where the premier XLCR was fitted with a set of Siamese exhaust pipes and was drenched in black, this updated version exhales through a set of separate and chromed tubes. The tank, seat and tail piece are all borrowed from the '77 version and are mated to a contemporary bikini fairing to complete the disguise.

I suppose that "replica" may not truly apply to this creation but it certainly bears a strong resemblance to the first XLCR from Harley-Davidson. For 1977 Harley had hoped to bring a new model to market that would enjoy some popularity among the fresh riders who were joining the ranks and buying mostly Japanese machines of that ilk. It was not a huge success but remains an iconic design for the fabled firm. This 1987 version uses a more modern EVO motor and frame while carrying the vintage tank and tail section of the first edition. Again taking styling clues from the '77 and '78 models this '87 carries a sport fairing that is familiar to the earlier units that were attached at the factory. Photo courtesy of www.bradsbikes.net

The legendary Norton marque has been around since 1901 and raced themselves into glory during the '20s and '30s. The 750 Commando came into view in 1968 and was an improved version of their previous 750 machines. Using that platform to build a replica of a racing motorcycle makes perfect sense and a great looking product. By adding the half-fairing up front and the solo seat and number plate out back you can almost hear the roar of the crowd as you swing by at 120 miles per hour. The solid disc brake on the front wheel did an admirable job of slowing the big Norton although its technology has been far surpassed with today's braking systems. All in all, this replica looks every bit as dominant today as it did in its heyday.

Only very limited numbers of the "yellow peril" Norton Production Racers were built at the Norton race shop. This particular example from 1971 is owned by Brad's Bikes and uses the larger European gas tank.

Like all the Production Racers, this one is based on a Norton Commando, and was indeed street legal - thus the name.

76

Much more than just a Norton commando with a fairing and tailpiece, the Production Racer came with true race bits like Akront rims, rear-sets with hand cut pegs, and re-valved front forks.

Though there were a few true race bikes built with full fairings (called the 750 Racer), the Production Racers came with this very "Cafe" fairing. The fairings and tail pieces were both designed in the Norton shop and manufactured locally.

More than just a 750 motor with polished covers, the Production Racers used a ported alloy head, larger intake valves, bigger carbs and increased compression to create a 70 horsepower 750, a bike that consistently won it's class on UK and European race-tracks of the day.

Rickman was one of the popular English chassis makers whose frames were meant to replace the factory frame and enhance the performance of the machine. A variety of frames and frame kits were sold to fit many different British engines of the period. Early frames were used for the scrambler class and later editions were seen on road race machines. The third version of their efforts was aimed at the street rider. This example of a Rickman frame has a Triumph Trident motor bolt-ed in place. The Rickman legacy usually carries brightly polished tubes blended with high quality fiberglass components. The "Metisse" name was developed by the Rickman's and was applied to several iterations of their machines. The definition of the word refers to a woman of multi-cultural background and they considered their creations to be used with a multitude of different motors hailing from various countries.

This 1972 Triumph-triple powered Metisse is one of only 10 built by Rickman. This particular example retains the Rickman gas tank, front fender, tail piece and original exhaust.

Rickman made frames and frame kits a variety of power plants, including both twin and triple-cylinder Triumph engines.

Rickman frames are nickle-plated Reynolds 531 tubing,m matched to a 40mm Rickman fork assembly, Lockheed Racing Brakes and Akront alloy rims.

DP Customs Black and White

Given few guidelines to build this bike for a client, DP Customs let their talent and skills do the rest. Needing to build a bike that rode well and was black and white was all that the buyer wanted so the DP crew went to work. The 1200cc Harley motor was given a good bath in black powder coat to replace the original chrome finish and the body panels now wear a matching set of hues. The rear cowl was formed from steel and took two attempts to get something they liked. The front forks were lowered and stiffened for a better ride and improved flow towards the rear of the chassis. Chainsikle rear sets help keep the rider's boots off the pavement and provide adequate grip for the soles of his footwear. The exhaust is brought to an end by the rectangular box seen under the frame. The resulting exhaust note is not as deep as expected and keeps the sound level to an acceptable level.

A pair of Progressive 970 shocks keeps the rear end of Black and White under control while providing comfort. Image by Strahmphoto

Using a 1200cc Harley-Davidson Sportster as their platform, DP Customs went to work to create this highly modified Café Racer for their client. Image by Strahmphoto

The rear cowl was formed using steel and required 2 attempts before the DP Customs crew was satisfied. Image by Strahmphoto

Rear sets via Chainsikle provide the rider with enough ground clearance and keep his boots firmly planted. Image by Strahmphoto

The hand formed exhaust ends up in the rectangular collector beneath the frame, looks great and keeps the volume to an appropriate level. Image by Strahmphoto

DP Customs Grabber Blue

Another creation from DP Customs in Arizona is this striking Grabber Blue Café Racer. Built around a Harley-Davidson 1000cc Ironhead motor and chassis, the rest of the cycle was built by combining hardware and original parts from across the globe. The tank hails from Benelli and the rear cowl and seat pan were hand formed by DP Customs. The DP team was also responsible for the crossover exhaust and for adding the tuck and roll upholstery to the solo saddle. Chainsikle was again tapped for the rear sets and DP created the clip-on bars to give the rider an aggressive riding posture. The Grabber Blue paint was a result of DP Customs being fans of Ford vehicles as the hue was chosen from the FoMoCo palette.

Based on a 1000cc Ironhead Sportster from Harley-Davidson the crew at DP Customs made some radical modifications to get Grabber Blue to its final stage. Image by Strahmphoto

After all of the factory hardware was removed DP Customs went to work creating new sheet metal for their effort and also fitted a range of new running gear to make it as functional as it is stylish. Image by Strahmphoto

DCM Framed XT500C   Owner: Stew Ross   Builder: Barry Murfett

Stew Ross is an enthusiastic cycle rider living in Australia and has quite a cadre of great cycles to choose from. Of them a few are built to be Café Racers like this DCM. The DCM stands for Dave Camier Motorcycles and he built the chassis in the '70s and '80s with the intention of them being used to joining the Café fray. This one is powered by a Yamaha XT500C motor and rolls on a rear alloy wheel laced to a TX500 hub. The front forks are from a TZ350A with lowers borrowed from an RD350 which permitted the use of disc brakes. The rear shock hails from DeCarbon in France adding another measure of exotic to the mix.

A Yamaha XT500C engine provides the motivation and the single-cylinder motor brings plenty of torque to the table. The alloy tank and tail section add another measure of Café Racer to the show while the rest of the machine is pure business. Image courtesy of Stew Ross

With a chassis from DCM playing host, the remaining assembly of this machine embodies the very spirit of a Café Racer and is currently being ridden in Australia. The race-inspired frame is the creation of Dave Camier Motorcycles and provides the owner with a stable platform on which to build his creation. Image courtesy of Stew Ross

Hellbilly Cycles has more of a history of building custom Harley-Davidsons but their skills allow them to take on many different styles of build. The owner of this Honda CX500 wanted something in the Café Racer style so Hellbilly took it to task. The factory saddle was replaced with a diminutive seating arrangement that also conceals the electronics under the hinged rear pad. An old school dash panel holds the required switches and warning lights and a tiny flyscreen deflects some of the air and insects from the rider's face. Exhaust pipes were truncated and wrapped with heat tape for sound and cooling improvements. K&N pods allow for free'r breathing and the lower bars put the rider in a fairly aggressive riding position. The matte black paint is offset by the copper hue and makes for a classic appearance on a contemporary machine.

An industrial grade switch panel has replaced the factory setup and looks far more rugged and at home on the matte black and copper CX500.

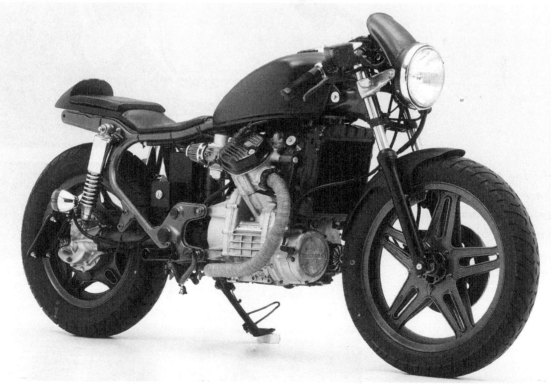

Known more for their customized Harley-Davidsons, Hellbilly Cycles has turned out a great machine that falls outside of their usual comfort zone with this Honda CX500 Café Racer. While a majority of the factory frame and running gear were left intact, modifications are everywhere as they eliminated weight and excess components for a cleaner look.

Far more Spartan than the original saddle the new pillion does double-duty as it hides the electronic components beneath the rear segment of the padded cushion.

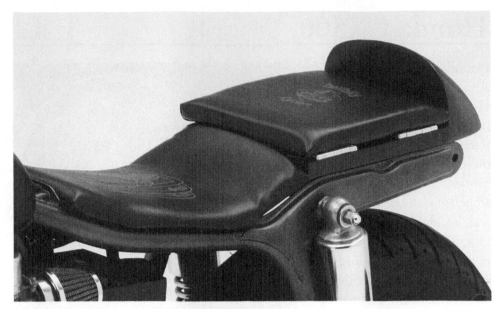

A set of classic clubman bars are joined by the tiny flyscreen and their combination puts the rider in a more aggressive position with only minimal protection from the wind.

Bringing added performance to the table thee K&N pods provide better breathing which results in sharper response when the throttle is turned.

1975 Honda CB200T

Looking through any Café Racer publication these days and you'll see repeated use of the Honda CB200 as a basis for a conversion. Fairly inexpensive to buy with a ton of available parts, you have one of the easiest projects you can find. The frame on this example was shortened and had all extraneous tabs removed before continuing with the build. High pipes from a Honda CL200 were used in place of factory low pipe and brakes from another Honda, the CB175 are found up front. Cosmetically the yellow and black paint scheme is really dramatic and brings a visual thrill to the typically staid machine. The foam intake keeps the air clean while improving flow. The low bars and Café Racer seating bring the theme to a close and adds the needed flair to complete the cycle.

Long distance touring was never the intended use for a Café Racer and the sparsely padded saddle on this version will make short work of your day on the road but looks right at home on this Honda.

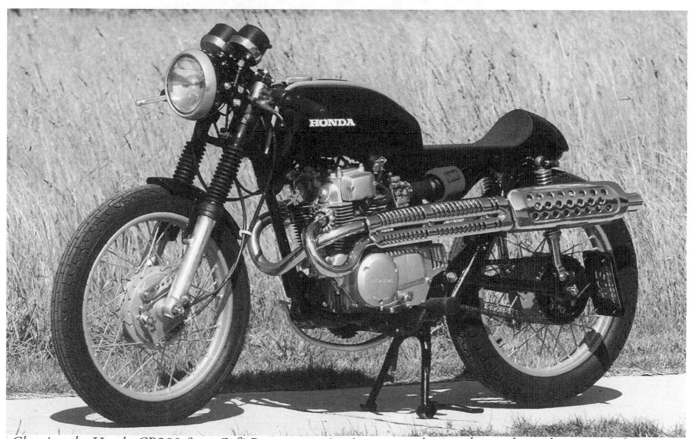

Choosing the Honda CB200 for a Café Racer conversion is an easy selection due to the wide array of alterations and available parts on the market. Steve has blended features of the CB and CL models along with the application of varying techniques to achieve the end result. The black and yellow paint scheme is another graphic element that makes this tiny machine stand out in a crowd.

The padded section running the length of the tank was a Honda original feature but the yellow bands that offset it from the gleaming black paint are Steve's choice to continue the black and yellow theme.

Using the high-pipes from a Honda CL200 of the same period changes the profile of the cycle without adding any undue noise or inconvenience.

Enhancing performance is always a goal when building a café Racer and by adding this better breathing foam air intake the results are easy to do and become obvious under power.

1978 Yamaha SR500

Walter Kuehn built this Yamaha for his friend Dennis and took about a year to complete the process. Based on the iconic Yamaha SR500, the machine was upgraded at every level including a White Brothers 12.5:1 piston and hotter cam inside the motor case. A Supertrapp exhaust handles the spent fumes. The tank and seat were formed by Evan Wilcox of Ukiah, CA and his work is world renowned for quality. By using the front forks of a different Yamaha, Walter was able to add the dual-disc brake setup to enhance braking on the nimble thumper. Custom mounts needed to be formed to attach the aftermarket rear sets to the chassis which was powder coated for durability and bright finish.

By combining the torque nature of the SR500 motor, red chassis and gold wheels this Yamaha has reached "classic" status among Café enthusiast.

Sadly Dennis would pass before spending much time on his fresh Café Racer but the legend of his machine lives on.

The SR500 makes a great starting point for a Café Racer project and this example was treated to all the upgrades for a really nice result.

Arch Motorcycle KR GT-1

As a longtime fan of motorcycles, Hollywood movie star, Keanu Reeves decided to take his next motorcycle to a new level. Working closely with Grad Hollinger of LA Chop Rods, the two combined their creativity and knowledge to produce the KR GT-1. It was a five year journey resulting in a truly unique machine. The heavily sculpted fuel tank was created from sections of alloy. The tail section is likewise an alloy piece, hand-shaped by craftsmen in Canada. The upside down super-moto front forks are from Ohlins that was shortened for use. A 32 degree rake with 5 inches of trail delivers comfort and stability on the fairly long chassis layout. The Harley motor was fine tuned for the application and exhales through a hand bent exhaust that sounds aggressive without being obnoxious. So satisfied with their efforts the team are planning on producing a small number of the machine that can be purchased by a rare few.

Created and built by the team of Keanu Reeves and Gard Hollinger the KR GT-1 is a handmade spectacle of technology and creativity. It required five years of planning to bring to life but the end result is beautiful and a joy to ride. Image credit: Mark Owen

Despite the length of the chassis the geometry provides taught steering while retaining comfort regardless of velocity. The gorgeous tank and tail section are sculpted from billet alloy and bring a new level of beauty to the aggressive machine. Image credit: Mark Owen

Chapter Seven

Café Racer Aesthetics

Key Components

When defining a Café Racer a few terms and visual traits come to mind. Regardless of whether the machine is powered by a British, Japanese, Italian or American motor it's the rest of the layout that will tell you it's a Café Racer. The most obvious changes will be made to the body panels including the fuel tank, tail section and saddle. Quite often a small bikini or sport fairing will also be used for both visual flair and to keep your face protected from the wind. Applying vivid colors and creative graphics to the material that forms these components will be highly personalized but

Inspired by the Ace Café in England these graphics are applied over the dark green powder coat and are continued on the front fender to complete the flow of art.

will tend to be created in the theme of the sport. As we already know there are no wrong answers to this question and only your imagination and check book will guide you to the design that best suits your needs. In the pages of this book alone you'll see a wide variety of themes being applied to an even wider variety of machinery. With any luck this diversity will allow you to come up with a theme and execution to make your own Café Racer just that, your own. The vendors and purveyors of the items spoken of in this book are listed in the Source Guide in the rear section of the pages. Consider it a finely tuned "yellow pages" for your café experience.

FAIRINGS AND BODYWORK

Taking a stroll down the rows at a local swap meet or via the internet will expose you to a dizzying array of available accessory bodywork for your new machine. By using "sport fairing" as an internet search you'll be astonished by the number of items being sold for that use. As always be sure to select the product that will fill your needs and retain safe operation of your cycle upon installation. Adding a really cool fairing that blocks your vision or the use of your lights does no one any good and will probably end up hurting you or someone else. Most of the sport or bikini fairings are simple affairs that bolt to the headlight brackets and add a nice visual reference and help to keep a small percentage of the wind and bugs off of your visor. The primary use for these compact and stylish fairings is to bring the Café racer feel to your ride although they won't provide storage or a place to mount a radio.

In addition to what you can find online or at the swap meets there are a few terrific companies that produce finely finishing fairings and bodywork that can be bought and used with little effort. Most are delivered in unpainted form allowing you to select the theme and hues to be applied once the items arrive. Air-Tech Streamlining has an extensive line of available options that are designed to work with a myriad of different machines. Formed using high-grade fiberglass the products are durable and easy to prepare for paint. Mounting them to your machine requires brackets to fit your exact chassis layout

A fast and easy way to add some art to the sides of your Café Racer would be to use these adhesive graphics that can be cut to fit nearly any surface. Courtesy of Economy Cycle

Analog Motorcycles has a keen eye for detail. To tie the motor trim pieces to the anodized wheels, they chose to have those same parts finished to a matching color for continuity.

To keep the theme of this highly modified Bimota up to date, Analog Motorcycles chose a compact instrument cluster from KOSO North America to give the rider all the pertinent data at a glance.

JCPak Bikes used a pair of Radiantz L.E.D. strip lights. The red section illuminates for braking, the same bulbs goes yellow to indicate a turn. Strips can be cut shorter as needed. Image: JCPakBikes.com

Leading the way on the custom Bimota is a headlight assembled using hardware from two different sources and a lamp assembly from Ebay with integrated turn signal bulbs.

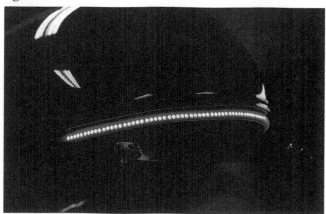

Analog Motorcycles built a unique tail section and fitted it with a single row of the Radiantz L.E.D. strip lights, shown here lit up to show that the brakes are being applied.

but again the lightweight material makes adding hardware a snap. Syd's Cycles, Inc. also carries a wide array of fairings and bodywork for Ducati models and has decades of experience in the arena. Hot Wing Glass makes a series of tail sections for your machine and their website gives enough information for you to order the correct item for your use.

If your tastes and budget have some extra room you can also opt for tanks and seat bases made by hand in alloy. This practice is not as fast as most of the pieces are made to order and made from scratch and as expected they are a bit pricier than the fiberglass components. VarnHagen Metalworks is in the business of producing such a line of parts and has several different designs to best suit your own application. They even offer a universal fit model that can be adapted to almost any chassis without too much effort. VarnHagen produces tanks and seat sections that can be matched to fit in design, bringing a more pleasing shape to the overall layout of your cycle. Another artisan toiling in the craft of hand shaping sheet metal into motorcycle trim is Evan Wilcox. Once again the nature of his art requires time and a higher cost than an off the shelf item and can be built to your exacting demands. He too can produce both seat sections and fuel tanks to meet with your exacting standards as long as you aren't in a hurry or on a strict budget. Framecrafters is another firm that can shape a fuel tank for your updated cycle using some very old school techniques. Once dimensions for the tank have been taken a form is made from steel tubing, then cardboard is used to create templates to fit the shapes of the frame. Sheet metal is then cut to match the templates and each piece gets welded in place to become a fuel tank. Final welding, grinding and finishing wraps up the process and brings a new dimension of unique to your creation.

Once you've taken delivery of your new fairing, you may want to add a different windscreen. Your reasons may be to bring some color to the equation or to alter the height and protection of the screen based on your riding style. Gustafsson Plastics, Inc. is well known for delivering a huge variety of screens to fit nearly any fairing whether new or vintage. They can also custom form one to match your existing fairing but again allow time and some extra expense for a one-off item. Zero Gravity also sells a nice line of windscreens that mount right onto your factory fairing. Different hues and configurations can be seen and ordered to meet with your specific needs.

In the early days of motorcycle customizing there was a company named Tracy that made one-piece bodies for motorcycles that were tailored to fit a specific machine. These graceful units bolted onto the chassis with little or no modification and blended the fuel tank, side covers and tail section into one single unit. The company has long since faded from view but if you are diligent and lucky they pop up on online shopping sites from time to time. They can also be found at swap meets on occasion but prepare to pay an extra dividend if you find one at all. They were never made in big numbers and had a way of disappearing as time went by. Odds are they can be found stuffed in barns and attics but knowing which hole to explore is your first hurdle.

Regardless of your design theme and intentions some research and digging will deliver whatever bits fit your cycle and will provide a personal expression of your intentions. As with most projects of this nature doing some advanced planning will permit you to narrow your search and result in locating exactly the items you need to bring your creativity to life.

Replacing the front fender with something more stylish and lighter in weight is another option with numerous examples molded in plastic or fiberglass on the market today.

HANDLEBARS AND CONTROLS

Regardless of how amazing your finished Café Racer looks, you're going to want it to be easy to steer and control the operations of the machine. By altering the handlebars that came from the factory you can easily make a big change to the way your cycle steers and responds to input. Using a lower set of bars will alter your riding stance but also give you a better feel when entering turns. The more radical clip-on bars literally attach to

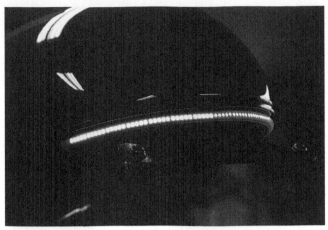

When flipping the switch to activate the turn signals, the same strip of red L.E.D. lights turn yellow to show the world your intentions and do it in high style.

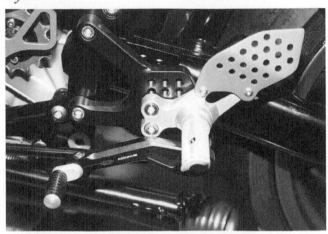

By delving deeply into the market of parts, Analog Motorcycles is always finding new suppliers for components. The rear sets on the Bimota hail from Rizoma and function flawlessly while looking great.

In keeping with their desire to build a truly unique machine, Analog Motorcycles drew up the plans for this fuel tank then had it hammered out of sheet metal for use on the Bimota.

Capture the café look with this Dunstall fairing from Airtech. Intended to fit nearly any motorcycle with a 7" headlight it can also be purchased with a wind-screen. Image: Airtechbody.com

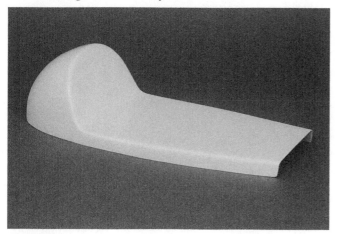

AirTechCR3502FL-tail provides the rider with a Café Racer seat made to fit a Honda CB350 when the standard fuel tank is installed. Image: Airtech/motobody.com

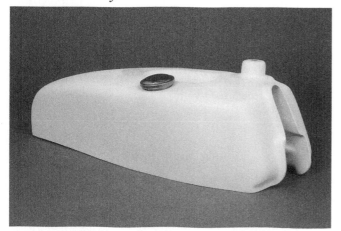

Created to fit any of Honda's iconic SOHC four-cylinder machines, the CR7503M also hails from Airtech. Image courtesy of Airtech/motobody.com

the upper sections of the fork tubes and give you a truly race-ready posture. Achieving the same goal without the same level of hardware modifications would be the use of Clubman bars. These models bolt into the OEM handlebar mounts and drop the grips and levers into a racing configuration. A less aggressive choice in the handlebar department would be the "superbike" bar. These bars tend to put the rider's hands at only an inch or so above the triple trees but provide a slightly more forward position. These bars provide an improved feel without causing back issues on a long ride. Nearly any form of handlebar can be had in chrome or gleaming black paint and as we will soon read there is a new selection of other finish options that await you.

Changing the grips and control levers is another facet of the plans you want to address if for no other reason than to improve the looks of the finished product. The comfort of the grip surface is more important if you plan on spending long hours at the handlebars and can also contribute to numbness of the hands if too hard a material is chosen. Style shouldn't trump comfort entirely but with a vast array of grips being sold you'll be sure to find a set that best suits your needs. Within the rubber category you'll still find an amazing choice between brands, styles and designs. Different compounds provide you with soft or firm grips and you can even see some molded in colors or with color accents with the standard black hue. To finish off the area a set of bar-end anti-vibration weights can be attached to the openings of your chosen handlebar.

Levers used to control the brake and clutch can also be changed to better meet with your needs. It may be a case of having smaller hands that have trouble reaching the factory levers. This can usually be corrected by using a set of levers that have a different contour, bringing the surface closer to the grips for an easier squeeze. Other considerations would be for adjustability and there are several models available that can allow you to adapt the settings of the levers with a simple twist of an adjustment knob at the lever itself. Catered more for the racing world they can still be applied to machines with a more serious nature or to simply add more features to your build for the ultimate in style.

Once you've modified the grips and levers on your machine you might consider dressing up or replacing the factory gauges. Assuming the faces of the instruments aren't so faded they can't be read you can always spiff up the housings by polishing or painting the stock fixtures or replacing their bodies with OEM items. If like so many older cycles that have suffered from years of outdoor storage you can take several paths to correct that situation as well. There are gifted artisans in the world who are capable of refinishing the faces of your gauges to original levels, bringing a new order to the day. Other choices include buying modern gauge faces and swapping the old for new. There are several outfits that cater to this method and by doing so you'll bring a fun feeling to your instruments while returning them to a functional status. Many of the same companies sell these items with colorful graphics and themes so that you can cater the change to your own tastes.

The third option would be to toss the old gear and purchase a set of high tech modern gauges. Once again there are several choices in that direction and one of the largest varieties I found was KOSO North America. Their catalog illustrates a diverse selection of arrays and something to fit nearly any need. Although there is plenty of data offered I'm not certain they will function with all

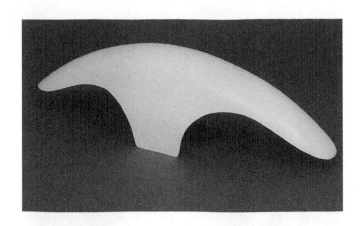

Modeled after the Ducati 900SS front fender this Airtech item will actually fit many motorcycles on the road and will bring a touch of nostalgia to those using it. Image courtesy of Airtech/motobody.com

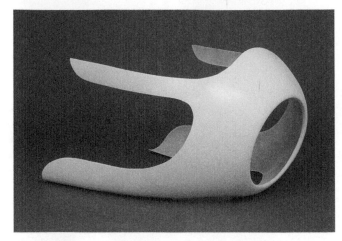

One of the many products offered by Air Tech Streamlining is this K2 Knoscher half fairing. It has an 8" headlight opening and is designed for universal fit. Image courtesy of Airtech/motobody.com

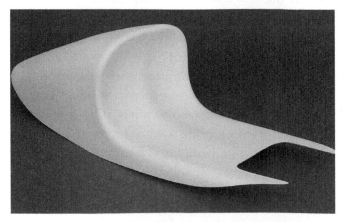

Looking every bit the tail section from a Harley-Davidson XR750 this item from Airtech will fit those as well as many other Café Racers. Product XR7502. Image courtesy of Airtech/motobody.com

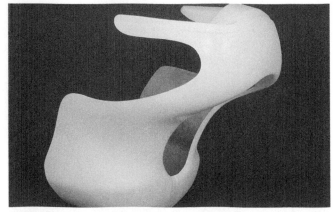

If you want to add a full fairing to your BSA or Triumph twin as well as several other machines, the TR16 model from Airtech will fill the bill. Image: Airtech/motobody.com

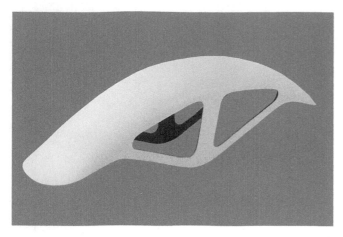

You can find many variations of aftermarket front fenders on the market today, but be sure to measure the distance between your fork legs before ordering to ensure proper fit. Courtesy of Economy Cycle

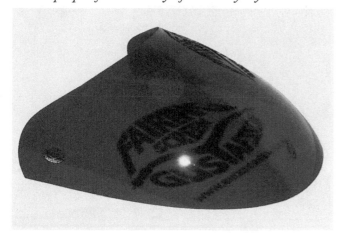

Gustafsson Plastics carries a line of factory replacement screens and can also mold one to meet your unique needs. A complete range of colors is available. Image courtesy of: Gustafsson Plastics, Inc.

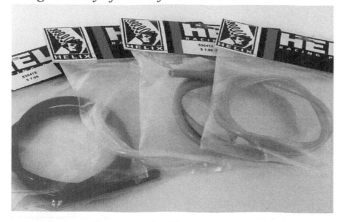

Your cycle will need a fuel line anyway so why not add a color-keyed style to accent the engine bay of your creation? All hues will work perfectly and can be cut to length with simple scissors. Economy Cycle

of the older machines and be sure to check for proper function before you buy. The same company also carries a big selection of turn signals and related accessories although many seem to be aimed at more modern machines.

The mirrors that came on your donor bike might still be shiny on at least one side but if yours are anything like mine they could use an upgrade. Once again you'll be faced with a myriad of choices in the mirror category but some will bring more style than others. Many different styles of mirrors are also available and of those, bar-end units harken back to the early days of the Café Racer. Within this narrow range you will still find a variety of choices but among the very best are the ones sold by Rizoma. This company carries nothing but high-end products for your motorcycle whether it's a Café racer or not. Among their offerings of bar-end mirrors, three models stand out. The Spy Q, Reverse Retro and Classic Retro all play a significant role in keeping you safe, within legal boundaries and adding a touch of style to your machine.

Another product in their lineup is the Fluid Tanks that are formed in billet and can be had in several hues to better compliment your existing design theme. We may not think much about the places our needed fluids are held but seeing these on your cycle will make lots of people think about it while wearing smiles of admiration.

LIGHTING

The universe of motorcycle lighting options is enormous and expanding faster than the universe we live in. As with all things Café you should do some research and decide what style you are trying to achieve before you log on to the internet or start flipping catalog pages.

Of course those are the two easiest ways to find what you're after but beware; both options provide you with nearly endless choices. You also need to consider the regulations in your state before removing the turn signals altogether as some states require them while others do not.

You can stay old school in your choices and stick to incandescent bulbs at all points or go the more modern method of adding L.E.D. equipped

96

lights. This fairly new Light Emitting Diode option has been around for a while but has finally trickled into the two-wheeled arena. Now that it's arrived you'll find yet another tremendous batch of options and choices to be made. The new L.E.D. style lights run cooler; produce more light and use smaller areas to do all three. One of the Café Racers in this book uses a really amazing tail light that hails from Radiantz LED Lighting.

Once installed, the lights will illuminate red for stopping and yellow for turn signal indication. The small diameter flexible design and immensely bright output make these an option that can be used on a lot of different machines.

A new style of turn signals incorporates the original look of the chrome housings with modern L.E.D. bulbs within. They are easy to install, typically use the same mounting points and wiring of the factory models and burn forever. They also produce far more light than the older incandescent bulbs adding a measure of safety while still looking true to form. If you have the inkling to replace the factory units with something sleeker there are a number of flush-mounted units on the market. Some of these will be equipped with the older style incandescent bulbs while others carry the latest L.E.D. light sources within. Again these are easy to attach using the factory wiring and can add a stylish look to your cycle or bring an air of stealth to the design due to their low profile execution.

Leading the way as you ride your new Cafe Racer will be the headlight and there too you are now faced with a huge selection of products on the open market. You can opt to simply clean up the existing headlight bucket and install a new bulb but I am betting you'll want to add something more to the game. Even replacing the existing ratty example on the bike with a newer and shinier copy will require some swap meet hunting or a trip to EBay but that is certainly an option if you are trying to retain the old world feel of your revised craft.

If you select a more contemporary path to light the way you will once again be inundated with choices on the open market. One company I

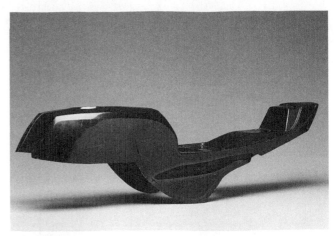

An unusual find is this one piece cover that installs on top of the factory tank of a Honda CB750. It can be painted to suit and removed with little fuss. Courtesy of Walneck's Classic Cycle Trader

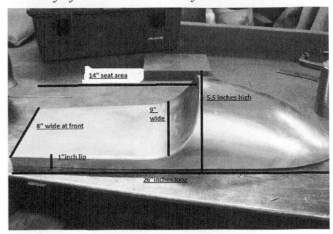

This illustrates the basic dimensions of the VarnHagen universal tail section and should give you enough info so you can tell if it will fit your application or not. Image courtesy: VarnHagen Metalworks

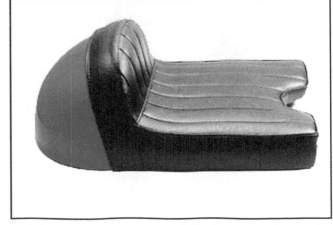

Sold as a tail section and saddle this nicely designed item comes from Clubman Racing Accessories and is one of many such items found on their website. Image courtesy of Clubman Racing Accessories

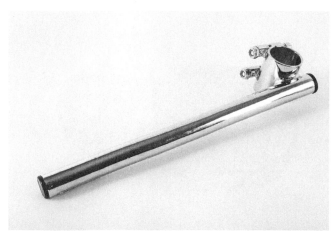

If you seek a more tradition method of lowering your handlebar location you can opt to attach clip-on bars to each of the fork legs with clamp-on units like this one sold by EMGO. Courtesy of Economy Cycle

These Clubman bars position your body much the same as a set of true clip-ons and bolt to standard risers.

Coating Specialties can also apply high-temp ceramic coatings in various colors to the exhaust portion of your project. The finish is durable and looks great for years to follow.

found doesn't specialize in the Café market but still presents an impressive array of lighting options. Street Fighter, Inc. is the company name and their website is a real treasure trove of lighting options along with a vast display of brackets and hardware to mount your new lighting. You'll even see many small bikini style fairings on the site giving you more choices in that direction. If you have a hard time making a decision maybe building a Café Racer isn't your bag.

Cruising that website or many others will provide you with endless options for lighting styles, sizes and output. You can replace your single headlamp with another single unit or go in the direction of a group of smaller units to comprise your total display. Round, oval, rectangular, if you want it you'll find it in an amazing array of finishes and price points. Like so many hobbies there is no end to how much money you can spend and that will only be dictated by common sense and your wallet. The Café Racer seen in the Gallery chapter of this book built by Analog Motorcycles created the headlight used by combining parts from two different vendors then locating the bulb assembly on Ebay. The entire piece looks like it came from a factory and adds yet another amazing detail to the machine.

Another terrific source for modern day parts for your Café Racer is Streetfighters, Inc. Of their catalog of lighting options their GSG headlamp assembly brings a touch of contemporary to your vintage ride or brings a modern bike closer to the future.

ALTERNATE FINISHES

Regardless of whether you've taken a radical path in your bodywork choices or stayed true to the original format, odds are the finished surfaces will be in need of freshening up.

If you are lucky enough to locate a "barn find" machine you'll be faced with very little of the factory surfaces intact and will need to refinish every inch of the machine. Of course the sheet metal portions of the cycle can be given a new coat of paint but as always, preparing the surface for the paint is as important as the application of the chosen hue. There is another cycle in the Gallery chapter that was painted using off the shelf spray paint but only after extensive efforts were taken to make sure the surface was clean and free of blemishes. The end result looks as good as anything I've witnessed.

Another direction that can be taken is to use powder coating for the surfaces of your cycle. This process bonds the finish to the metal using heat and results in a highly durable yet beautiful finish that will look great for years to come. It is often used to coat frames, motors and wheels but can be applied to any metal that can withstand a 400 degree baking process. A huge palette of colors and finishes is on tap and seems to grow every day. I was able to capture some images at Coating Specialties and they have 400 colors on hand but told me there are 1000s of other choices to be selected from.

For the exhaust, and any components on your cycle that get hot, high-temperature ceramic coatings provide another way to finish the parts, making them look great and carry that appearance for years.

Anodizing is another high-tech method of finishing parts but has its limits as to what types of metal it can be applied to. A nice expanse of colors can be chosen and the application needs to be done at a professional location. Anodizing is usually applied to aluminum and alloy materials and can add a really nice dimension to your project.

Some of the polished case covers on an older

To reduce the vibrations felt at the handlebars, you can easily insert a set of these anti-vibration bar end weights and quickly reduce or eliminate the numbness often experienced while riding. Economy Cycle

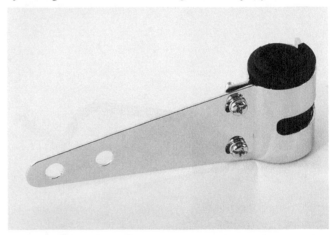

For headlight mounts you can reuse the OEM brackets or add a pair of chrome brackets. They will attach to any tube diameter and can be bent to fit the headlight of your choice. Economy Cycle

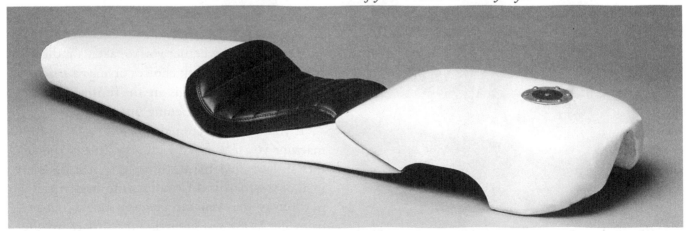

This two-piece affair replaces the factory tank and seat of your Harley and brings a new level of sport to the game. Produced in high quality fiberglass it is both strong and light weight. Courtesy of Walneck's Classic Cycle Trader

Your machine may already have a set of chain adjusters at the rear end so why not dress up the detail with a set of anodized units? Courtesy of Economy Cycle

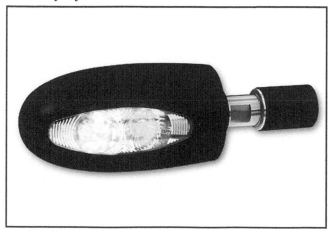

Turn signal options have grown exponentially while the lights themselves have shrunk. Kellerman offers these bar-end models which deliver high intensity from a very compact design. Image:Streetfighter, Inc.

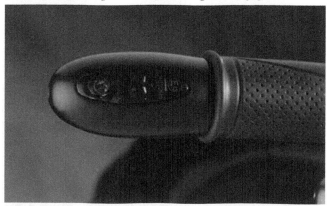

Another option for bar-end signals if offered by there Kellerman Micro 1000 DF units built with bright L.E.D. bulbs for a enhanced visibility. Image courtesy of Streetfighter, Inc.

machine will have taken on a lot of crud and corrosion during its lifetime and some may be able to be saved without replacement. A light sanding with fine grit sandpaper allows you to remove any of the big chunks of trouble and reveal the depth of corrosion on the surface of the piece. As long as the surface appears to be fairly smooth and unblemished you can simply use metal polish to return the cover to its former glory. Start off using a stout compound and move towards less abrasive polish to achieve that perfect sheen. Once polished you can apply a coat of clear to preserve the finish or simply plan on returning to the scene to maintain the restored luster later.

GRAPHICS

The decision to add graphics to your cycle's ensemble is a personal one. As with every other step in the process can be chosen to work with your overall theme for the bike - contrasting colors or complimentary accents or whatever seems to fit. Once a selection has been made there are a variety of methods to achieve those goals.

If you are talented or know someone who is gifted in the art of applying paint to a metal surface that's one way of adding art and graphics to your scoot.

Once the desired art has been sprayed into place a clear coat will follow to provide a smoother finish as well as protecting the design beneath. Careful wet sanding and buffing of the final layer will add depth and clarity to your design and allow it to stay sharp and colorful for years.

One of the newer trends in graphics application has been vinyl. The material can be cut into whatever shapes needed then applied to the surface of the machine. One of the benefits of this process is that you can alter the design at any time by removing one set of vinyl and replacing it with another. There are companies that can wrap entire cars in a printed piece whether it be your favorite sports team or your company's logo. Using this method would be useful for a fuel tank or tail section but wrapping an entire motorcycle is not an option due to the moving parts and heat of the engine and exhaust. As creative as the technology is there are some drawbacks. An easier choice for adhesive graphics is a set of pre-printed art. These can be found in your choice of styles, colors and length and all can be cut to fit the location of your selection.

If you chose to use alloy bodywork to complete your Café Racer you can either leave it in its original form or have it sealed with a clear coat to preserve the raw form while preserving the consistency and saving you from constant upkeep of the unprotected metal.

REFINISHING FACTORY TRIM

If your project involves retaining some of the factory panels and related name badges, odds are the badges will have lost some of their luster due to time and weather. Your first choice would be to try and locate OEM replacements online or at swap meets but they are not a common find and are often in as bad a condition as the ones you hope to replace. Nearly every example of the name badges are molded in plastic so any use of high heat applications are out of the question. Using an applique to bring back the original gleam is a choice too but getting the material to stay in place over time is a real challenge. This method is also highly dependent on the surface being prepped and free of any debris or irregularities.

The easiest method requires some time and a steady hand. If the badges can be removed without damage, do that first to protect the panels beneath from damage. Once free of the mounting panels use a small grit sandpaper to remove surface issues and to provide a smooth surface for the paint. If the background of the badge is black it's better to recoat that before moving to the shiny silver or gold that will be applied to the badge's type. With the black areas corrected you can use a small brush to apply a coat of silver, gold or any hue you desire to the wording on the badge. Factory finish was typically silver or gold and while those are acceptable choices for refinishing there's no one saying you can use a color that will contrast or compliment the colors used on the rest of the cycle's panels and frame. A coat of clear will once again help to add brilliance and preserve the newly applied finish.

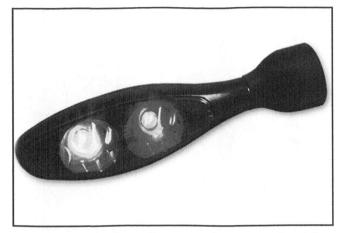

Replace your bulky stalk mounted turn signals with a set of sleek Kellerman Micro 1000 DF units that are built with super bright L.E.D. bulbs. Image courtesy of Streetfighter, Inc.

Bar-end mirrors are a throwback to the early days of the Café Racer but now attach more solidly while providing a clear view rearward. Image courtesy of Streetfighter, Inc.

A great way to add a safer, brighter turn signal to your mount while retaining the factory look is to use a pair of L.E.D. units. These modern lights provide superb output and use the OEM wiring.

Streetfighter, Inc. sells a huge line of lighting and related accessories for your motorcycle, and the GSG Round headlight is only one among the many. Stylish and rugged it also delivers plenty of light as you continue riding for miles after the sun goes down. Image courtesy of Streetfighters, Inc.

Although they're better known for their chassis designs and construction Framecrafters can also form fuel tanks into any shape needed and this is just one example that was in the shop the day of my visit.

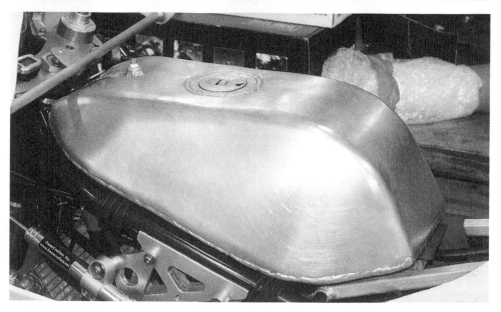

Another example of their craftsmanship being applied to a fuel tank, this is the second unit being used to build a race bike at Framecrafters.

Once they have formed a steel tube buck for the assembly, cardboard is used to determine the required shapes of the sheet metal that will be used to create a new fuel tank at Framecrafters.

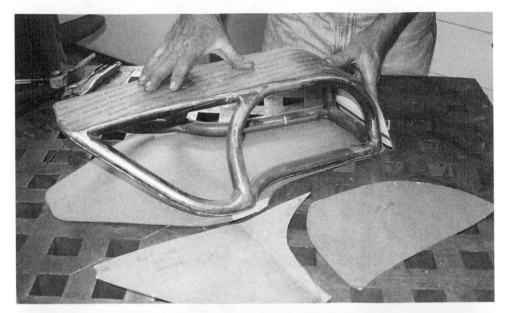

Placing the cardboard shapes onto the steel frame beneath they can be sure that when the sheet metal is cut to the same proportions it will fit before being welded to become another original piece from Framecrafters.

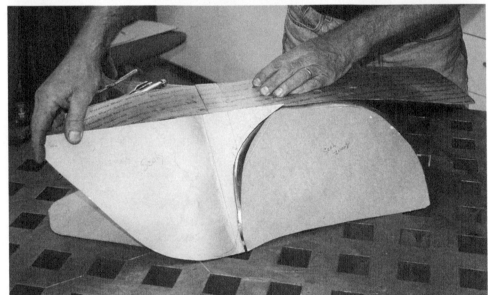

After all of the sheet metal panels are shaped and welded in place, all the welds are sanded smooth. The finished tank can be painted, or leave in its raw state before mounting.

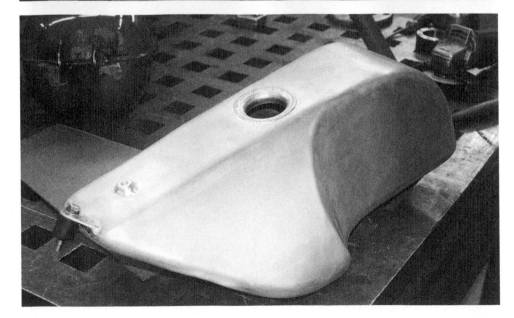

Odds are if you're donor cycle has been sitting around for a few decades the factory badges will look something like this and really hurt the resulting machine that you're building.

After some gentle sanding to remove the old finish you can reapply a fresh coat of gold, followed by clear coat to return the original luster to the side covers of your machine.

"M" bars from Norman Hyde are just one of thousands of handle bar options to consider for your new or vintage Cafe Racer.

Years of exposure will often diminish the original gleam from the aluminum case covers, but a bit of time and elbow grease can return them to a higher level of shine as long as the surface wasn't too badly pitted.

Reservoirs for clutch and brake fluid don't have to be plain and plastic. Available in a variety of colors, these cut-from-billet reservoirs add detail to the bars or chassis. Image courtesy of Rizoma

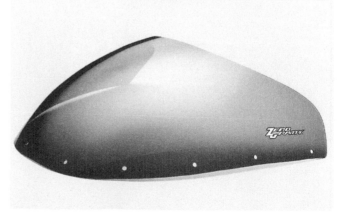

Depending on which sport fairing you choose, Zero Gravity makes a series of screens in different colors to change the appearance of your fairing with ease. Image courtesy of Zero Gravity

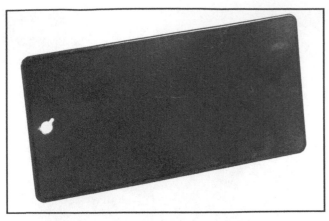

To satisfy your wilder side, Coating Specialties has a wide selection of bright powder-coat colors that can be applied to the metal surfaces of your project including this Candy Purple.

Coating Specialties can create a fade by blending two different colors to give a unique look to your project.

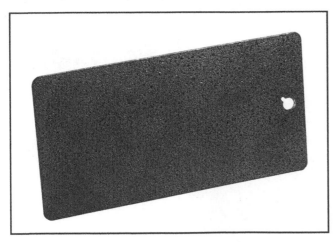

In addition to an array of smooth and glossy finishes, Coating Specialties offers a nice range of textured finishes like this Copper Vein.

Here the lower fins have been eliminated, the area polished, then masked off during the powder coating process. The net result is a cylinder with nice contrast between the color and the polished areas.

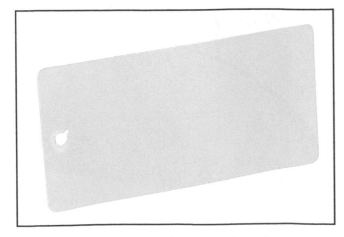

If you have chosen to go the route of powder coating for the refinish on the metal portions of your Café Racer you'll find 1000s of hues at your fingertips and Coating Specialties can apply any of them.

Or you can opt to have CS cut and polish only the edges of the fins as shown here. Thousands of colors are available and the powder coated finish will not be affected by engine heat.

Under the Pro Grip banner you'll find a huge selection of grips including these all-black units with a nicely textured surface for adequate control regardless of the weather. Economy Cycle

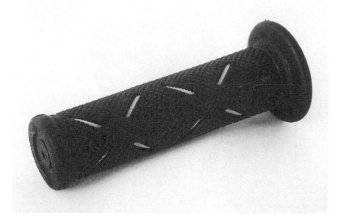

Another variant in the Pro Grip series are these that add a subtle accent of color to the surface material bringing style to the already functional equation. Courtesy of Economy Cycle

Renthal is another name that has been in the motorcycle world for decades and they offer a nice selection of grips to today's riders including these black models in a "firm" composition. Courtesy of Economy Cycle

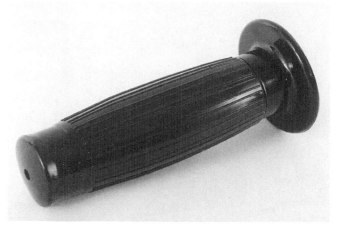

For anyone who has ridden motorcycles long enough these Dixie grips will look like an old friend. Still sold today in brand new form it will add a touch of nostalgia to you modern day ride. Economy Cycle

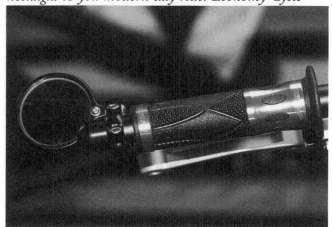

Analog Motorcycles chose to install a pair of grips in the matching shade of copper to accent the rims and also added the bar-end mirrors that were so popular on the early café Racers.

Not only are these grips molded in a nice shade of gray but are also made using a "soft" compound for added comfort. Courtesy of Economy Cycle

Retaining more of the iconic look, the Rizoma Classic Retro bar-end mirror combines dark and light finishes with a crystal clear mirror for a great view of what you just passed. Image courtesy of Rizoma

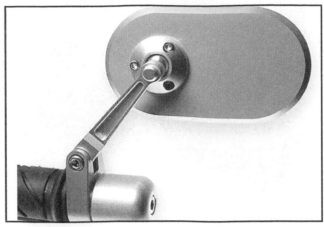

Bar-end mirrors are a throwback to the early days of the Café Racer but now attach more solidly while providing a clear view rearward. Image courtesy of Streetfighter, Inc.

Compact yet highly stylish, these Reverse Retro bar-end mirrors will allow you to see what's behind you and look great at the same time. Image courtesy of Rizoma

Changing over to bar-end mirrors is a simple matter when choosing any of the Oberon clamp-on models...

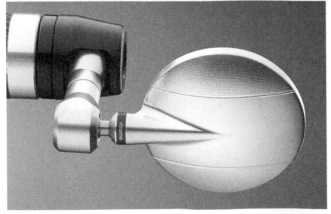

Another variant in Rizoma's extensive catalog is the Spy R bar-end mirror. The diminutive size still keeps you within the law while providing a sharp look at the world behind you. Image courtesy of Rizoma

... available in numerous shapes, and various colors including black and silver. Images courtesy of Streetfighter, Inc.

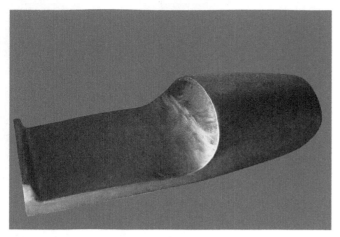

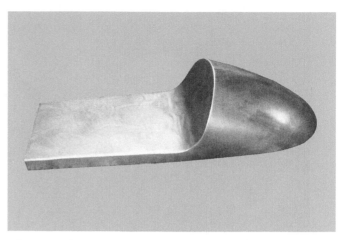

Based in Illinois and highly experienced in metal working, VarnHagen Metalworks offers seats and tail sections for the Honda CB550 and 750 chassis. While this model can be ordered as shown, you can also have VarnHagen create one that matches your specific taste and motorcycle. Image courtesy of VarnHagen Metalworks

If you prefer something a little shorter for a sportier look VarnHagen Metalworks also offers this version of their tail section for Honda CB550 and 750 models. Image courtesy of VarnHagen Metalworks

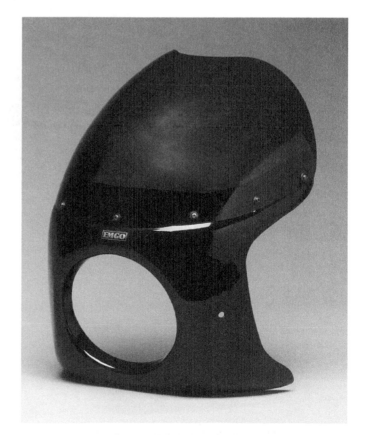

Purchased at a swap meet, this bikini fairing mounts to the headlight, provides some protection from the wind and brings a touch of style to your Café Racer.

This sport fairing by Emgo can be found readily on several online locations and is fairly easy to locate on Ebay as well. It mounts to the headlight and adds a bit of flair to your creation.

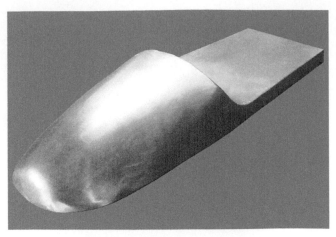

In their attempt to satisfy every need of the Café Racer, VarnHagen also sells this tail section with a lower profile as shown.
Image courtesy of VarnHagen Metalworks

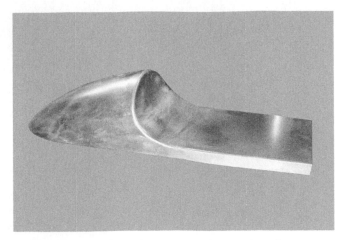

This universal-fit tail section is designed to fit a variety of bikes. Image courtesy of VarnHagen Metalworks

If you plan on spending some time on the open road aboard your Café Racer this Tracy fairing includes a taller windscreen for added protection from the wind.

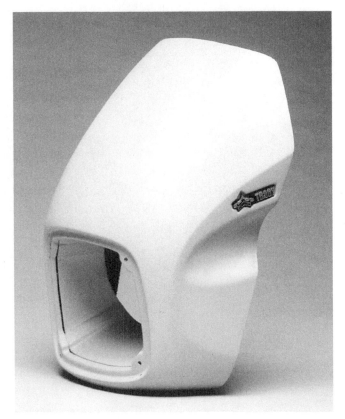

Molded in a single piece including the windscreen, this Tracy fairing leans more towards the quarter mile than it does the highway but still provides a measure of protection.

Chapter Eight

Café Racer Tools

Can't Fix Stuff Without 'em

As we mentioned in the first chapter building a Café Racer is probably not your first two-wheeled venture. Like most of us who have owned a variety of machines through the years, our tool boxes are chock full of the daily requirements in the hardware division. Wrenches, screwdrivers, socket sets and who knows what else has accumulated in those pull-out drawers. The collection of tools you currently own will more than likely suffice when turn-

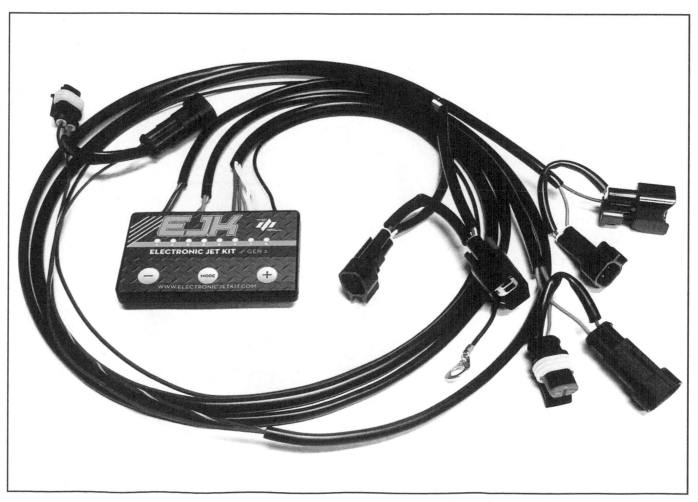

Dobeck Performance has created a series of modules that are used to upgrade your cycle's existing EFI system without remapping the numbers that are installed by the manufacturer. Their EJK can be ordered in your choice of Gen3 or Gen 3.5 and their website will tell you what module will best suit your needs. Image:Dobeck Perf.

*At right: Making life easier than in the past, a brake
bleeding kit like the Mityvac reduces the chore of
removing unwanted air form the brake lines a breeze
by pulling the air out at the bleeder.
Courtesy of Economy Cycle*

ing your attention to a specialized craft like a
Café Racer but in my journey I found a few that
would make worthy additions to your war chest
or tool box. As always we can make common
tools achieve things they aren't meant for but
acquiring those that are geared specifically
towards certain actions will enhance the experience and make the task a far easier process.

All of the items spoken of here are fairly
inexpensive so justifying their purchase for a single use won't break the bank or your arms when
the significant other finds
out you bought another
tool. Using them more
than once will quickly
amortize the purchase and
make you wonder how you
got along without them for
so long.

As a helpful reminder,
John at Economy Cycle
told me that far too often
people order new parts and
once received and taken
home they realize they
need a different tool to
complete the task of
replacing the old. When
ordering new parts, ask the
seller if they have any suggestions for installation. It
may require spending a few
more dollars on a tool but
when the time comes to
swap the parts you'll be
happy you did and without
waiting for the needed tool

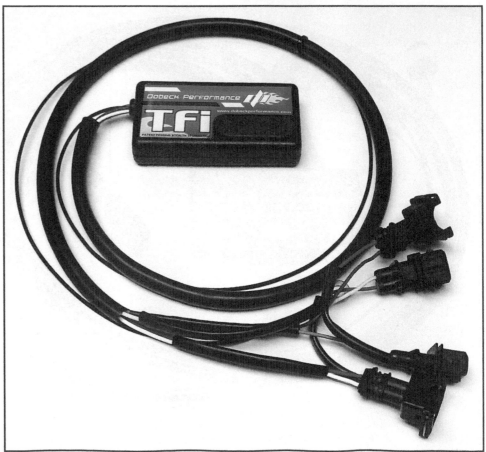

*This 2 channel TFI module allows for greater flexibility when installing in con-
junction with your existing EFI setup. Image courtesy of Dobeck Performance*

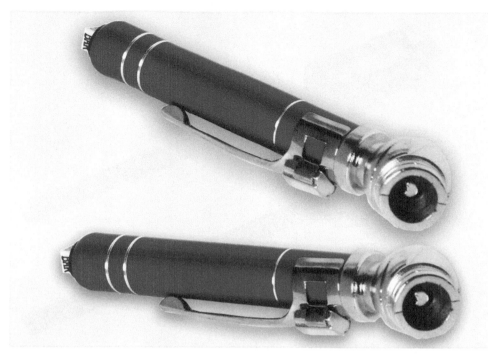

By keeping your tires properly inflated you'll prevent a rash of problems and your Café Racer will handle better. Using a simple air pressure gauge will tell you how much pressure your tire has and how much has to be added. This unit is small enough to fit in your riding suit pocket. Courtesy of Motor Cycle Center MCC

When replacing or even inspecting your disc brake pads, this brake spreader makes it easy to push the pistons all the way back into their bores. Courtesy of Economy Cycle

to arrive as the fresh parts stare at you from the workbench.

If you've selected an older cycle to be the platform for your Café Racer, odds are the inside of the fuel tank has gone from pristine silver to something far less attractive. Rust, corrosion and an entire league of nonsense can build up inside the walls of the fuel storage container and will need to be corrected before filling with fresh fuel and riding away.

By leaving debris and rust in the tank, those stray substances will eventually break free and enter the delicate system that keeps your cycle running. If you've ever had the pleasure of rebuilding a set of carbs due to excess dirt built up inside you'll know the value of keeping the fuel tank clean. In the past you were faced with only a few options to cleanse the inner walls of the tank but today we have a much neater and faster method at our avail. Caswell Fuel Tank Sealer achieves the same task as before but requires only two steps to reach the finish line.

The Caswell sealer uses a modern blend of Phenol Novolac Epoxy to permanently seal the inside of the tank with a corrosion and chemical resistant surface that will last for years if not forever. Another wonder of today's science the process is easier than before with a result that will astound even the skeptic in the crowd.

After cleaning the inside of the tank using acetone you simply pour the sealer in, splash the material around to properly cover every inch of the interior. Once distributed pour out the remaining fluid and allow the tank to dry overnight.

Obviously other precautions are suggested to ensure the best results and the product provides you with a comprehensive list of steps to deliver a quality end product. It's not horribly expensive and will certainly cost less than replacing the tank, especially if you are using an OEM unit that is hard if not impossible to replace.

The caliper has been around for decades but the advent of digital technology makes them more precise and easier to read than ever before. You can use a caliper to measure the outside diameter of tubing or the inside opening of any fitting prior to installation. Having components that fit together makes life a whole lot easier and it's better to check before attempting to attach two items into one. Courtesy of Motor Cycle Center MCC

When working with an older machine any changes to the exhaust or intake on the motor will require you to re-jet the carbs. When you buy an upgraded exhaust for a fuel injected Ducati this fuel injection mapping unit is part of the kit. Install the new pipe, plug in the unit and let your cycle's onboard computer learn the new way of delivering fuel for optimum performance. Courtesy of Motor Cycle Center MCC

When redoing the wire harness on your machine or simply updating a few cracked and broken connections this kit provides everything you'll need regardless of the electric connections you face. Courtesy of Economy Cycle

Cleaning and sealing the inside of your fuel tank got a whole lot easier. A quick acid bath before the application of the epoxy sealant will deliver a tank lining as good as new with little effort on your part. Courtesy of Economy Cycle

Another fairly common upgrade when rebuilding a motorcycle of any style would be to inspect and possibly replace the clutch plates. As they age they get a glaze on the surface and often won't function as designed once the surface of the plates gets marred with the ages of time and abuse.

Once the oil has been drained from the motor and the cover is taken off the clutch basket you'll need to loosen and remove the bolts that hold the assembly in place. The process of achieving this is made far easier by using a tool that holds the spinning basket in position as you twist the fasteners loose. EBC makes just such a tool, making life a lot easier. It simply slips over the notches on the clutch basket and using the fixed handle you can keep the clutch assembly from spinning as you break the bolts free. Certainly beats jamming a screwdriver into the space between the basket and cases and prevents damage from the half-witted method.

Another weapon in the clutch removal battle is the clutch holding tool from Motion Pro. Once in position you can tighten the jaws to hold the clutch basket secure allowing the needed work to commence without issue. It can also be used on sprockets as well thus adding another reason to add one to you arsenal.

Another crucial step when building your café Racer will be to take time to be sure that the brake components are up to spec before taking to the streets. Since a disc brake system uses hydraulics to operate, the pads and piston are often backed with pressure from the fluid making them difficult to ease back into their contracted position. To facilitate the replacement of the brake pads, using a brake spreader brings new pleasure to the process. Once in position you simply turn the handle to squeeze the inner pad and piston into a retracted location allowing you to slip the assembly free for inspection and replacement of the pucks if deemed necessary.

Once you access the inner workings of the brake system and especially if you replaced pads, lines or any portion of the system you'll need to remove excess air from the lines to deliver precise stopping. There are tools on the market now that make the process far easier than the old days of slowly pumping the brake lever, checking for air and repeat, often. The Mityvac is just such a tool and by following the included instructions you'll be able to bleed your bakes in far less time than before. If attempting

Checking to make sure your ignition system is providing the needed spark is crucial when tuning your Café Racer and this device allows you to easily check the strength of the spark by gauging how far a gap it will jump. Courtesy of Economy Cycle

These pocket calculators from Mikuni make the job of jetting and tuning a Mikuni waaay easier than it ever was before. Courtesy of Economy Cycle

to rebuild the master cylinder it will bring a new level of joy to the process by using a pair of snap ring pliers to remove the retaining ring that lives inside the housing. These pliers allow you to easily reach inside the master cylinder and remove the c-clip with ease. The cramped space within the housing makes other methods challenging and the pliers simply reach in and take hold, letting you compress the clip and lift it out of the grooves.

When using an older machine as the basis of your build you will probably find that the electric look has become brittle, dirty and will more than likely have a few of the multi-pin connectors in need of replacement.

Lucky for us we can now buy sets of these connectors that come with a variety of connector configurations permitting us to easily swap out the old, crusty bits with fresh, clean replacements. When reattaching any new connectors to your new wire it's important that the bond between the wire and connector is done properly and nothing works better than a ratcheted crimper tool. The jaws of this device offer several choices of size to

Another tool to eliminate frustration when removing the c-clip deep inside your master cylinder is this set of pliers that allows easy access and removal of the pesky ring. Courtesy of Economy Cycle

deliver the precise amount
of crimp without going too
far or not far enough.
They also prevent any
over-crimping when set-
ting them to bind the
required components.
Once again, not an expen-
sive tool but one that can
be used for a variety of
wiring needs not just those
on your cycle.

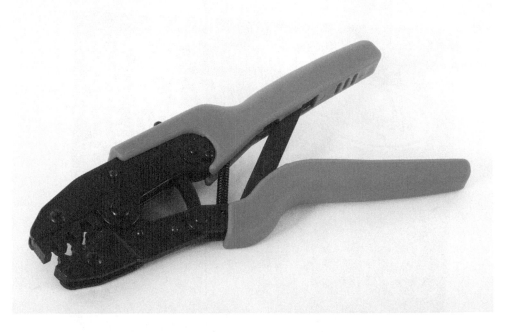

When checking the
ignition to be sure of adequate spark and function
another valuable asset is
the ignition system tester.
By testing the gap that
your provided spark can traverse the stronger the
signal of the electrical system. A strong spark
means cleaner burning and improved output.

*Providing a solid connection between the wire and
connectors used on the electric system is key and the
use of this ratcheted wire crimper delivers precise
crimping without the fear of over or under crimping
the junction. Courtesy of Economy Cycle*

If you've chosen the path of installing new
or well cleaned carburetors you'll need to tune
them to meet with the factory specs to gain the
biggest advantage offered
by replacing or cleaning
them. A must have for
anyone working with
Mikuni carbs is the Tuning
Manual and its associate
the Pocket Tuner which
allows you to determine
what main jet will function
best for your application.
Years of trial and error
have gone into creating
these valuable items and
are a great addition to your
collection if you plan on
doing any carb work at
home.

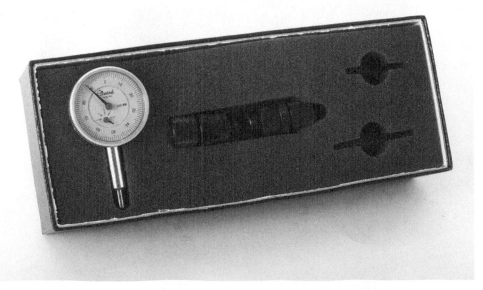

The use of a timing
gauge will provide you with
the correct timing of your

*Dial Gauge timing kit for inspection and adjustment of ignition timing. Gauge
will work with the engine in the frame on RD's, R5, RZ's, and most bikes.High
quality, high precision instrument by Central Tools. 5.0mm range, .01mm
increments, 0-100 sweep reading. Courtesy of Economy Cycle*

You can't have too many wrenches in your tool box, these combination wrenches from Motion Pro are easy to handle and the size of each is clearly marked. Image courtesy of Motion Pro

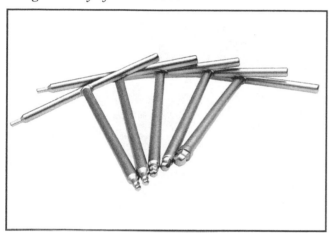

This set of T-Handle hex wrenches from Motion Pro will make the time changing those pesky fasteners a breeze no matter how tight they are. Image courtesy of Motion Pro

With its digital output this air pressure gauge from Motion Pro is easy to read, and reaches more obscure valve locations with its extended nozzle. Image courtesy of Motion Pro

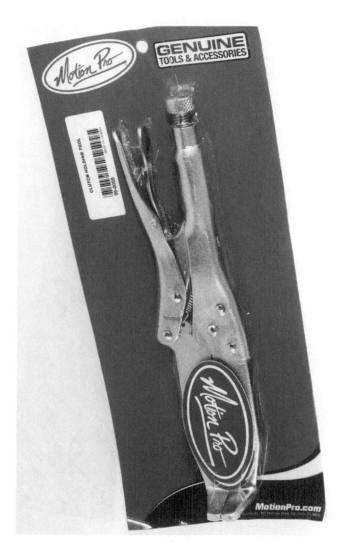

If you've ever replaced a clutch assembly without one of these you soon learn how foolish you were to try. Today's tools are designed to make a task simpler and remove irritation from the process, and this is one that rates high on the list. Courtesy of Economy Cycle

motor's internal for optimum performance and fuel mileage. A poorly timed engine will not even get close to its peak output thus robbing you of fun when there's a simple way of correcting any issues prior to hitting the streets. Not an impossible tool to learn but if you aren't confident of your skills turn to the experts for guidance and assistance.

The tools suggested here are among the 100s of choices you face when adding to your tool box. As we know you can spend 1000s of dollars on tools and if that's your plan and with-

If you enjoy the aggravation of removing the clutch components from the basket then by all means don't add one of these to your tool box. However if you prefer saving time and frustration feel free to try this easy to use tool. *Courtesy of Economy Cycle*

in your budget we're not here to stop you. The more practical method is to only purchase the tools you need for the job with hopes of needing them again down the road. Even if you only need a tool for a one-time application it's better not to scrimp on the price because odds are a less expensive tool won't do the job as well as hoped, forcing you to buy another. Buying a quality tool once is always better than buying several cheaper units to achieve the same goal. Of course none of your pals will want to borrow the cheap tools so there may be one advantage

Combining the features of the iconic box end wrench with the convenience of the ratchet these hand tools make a great addition to your collection of hand tools and are easily found at many retailers.

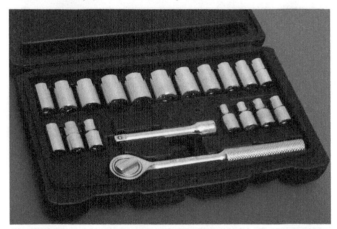

No garage builder can function without a set of sockets - they can be had in any number of sizes and drives to fit nearly any hex head fastener.

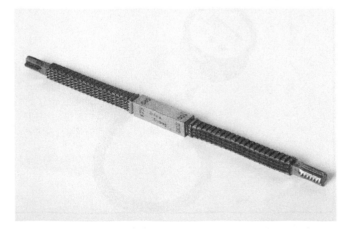

This tool is great for cleaning up the damaged threads on various male fasteners when you don't have the correct die.

Another way to improve the performance of your modern Ducati is to install an upgraded throttle body assembly. Each assembly is designed for use on a specific model but attaches directly to the existing motor layout to deliver improved output with far less hassle than in the old days. Courtesy of Motor Cycle Center MCC

Among the numerous items found in the Motion Pro catalog this set of bearing pullers will simplify the act of removing old bearings from nearly any location on your Café Racer chassis. Image courtesy of Motion Pro

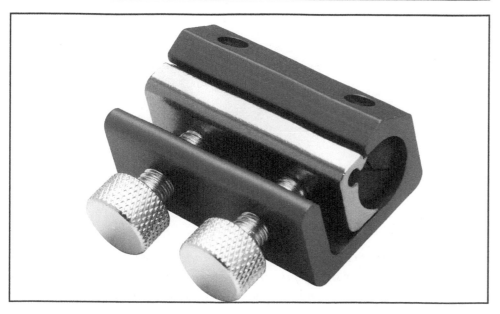

Keeping the various cables on your bike lubricated is now far easier with the use of this cable lube tool. Image courtesy of Motion Pro

to going that route. I would also avoid going the orange hammer method when assembling your Café Racer. While it looks great on TV parts that need to be hammered into place don't belong together in the first place.

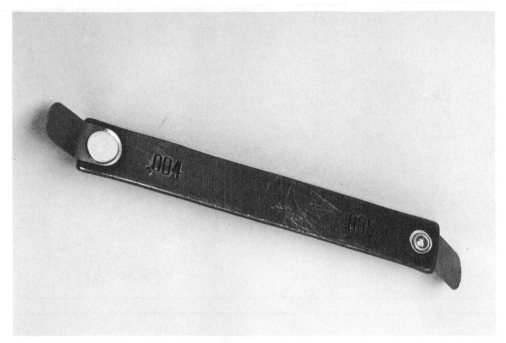

When checking and adjusting the gaps in your valve train a set of these gauges will make life much easier. The angled heads and non-slip handle makes them easy to use. Courtesy of Motor Cycle Center MCC

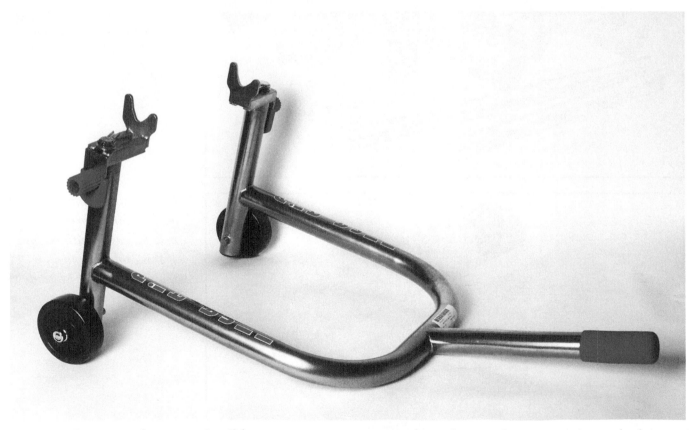

The use of a universal rear stand will bring great joy to anyone working alone in their garage. Any cycle chassis with a two-sided swingarm can be held in place safely by simply pivoting the stand under the rear and lifting. Much greater access to the chassis is attained with only a minimum of fuss. Courtesy of Motor Cycle Center MCC

Chapter Nine

Build #1

Circle K Kustoms Café Conversion

After completing their CB200 Café Racer conversion to a satisfied level of success, Richard and his friends decided to take things to the next level. With the goal of producing more examples of the Café Racer for friends and clients they chose to organize their talents into a more formal organization. After several meetings of the minds the name Circle K Kustoms was arrived at. Richard considers himself a "co-captain of a loose knit fraternity" and wanted to give a nod to Kurt

Looking at this finished bike, it's hard to believe that they started out with the two piles of junk seen on the next page. All a matter of skill, planning, patience and careful execution (including the nice paint job).

and his many talents. This is why the "K" in Circle K came to be. Even the quirky misspelling of "Kustoms" was intended to add another level of intrigue to this crafty group of builders. With the new identity settled they then took on the task of choosing their first "official" project. It would take several additional gatherings and discussions before choosing the iconic Yamaha RD350 "the little giant killer" for a starting point. The legend of the RD family is well known among fans of two-wheeled fun so it wasn't a tough choice to make and parts were readily available to convert their machine into what they envisioned.

Drawing inspiration from the historic racing bikes of old they chose to utilize the traditional trappings of those machines while upping the ante with modern conveyances. The fairings, seats and bodywork were all a part of the attraction so various components to achieve that change were tracked down and added to the growing stack of needed bits to begin and complete the conversion with only minimal delays. The second motivation for this build was a rapidly approaching show that would be a perfect place to debut their new company and creation. With only 31 days remaining before the Rockerbox event in Milwaukee the talented team would now face the added pressure of time. Without wanting to sound like one of today's "reality" shows that always seem to put the televised efforts under the clock but that's what Circle K Kustoms chose to do.

To suggest their starting platform was a basket case would be kind. Two mostly disassembled and partially incomplete machines, one an RD and the other an RZ would be used to create their modern Café Racer and set the bar fairly high even for a group with nearly limitless skills. If their plans were to simply bolt on some fairings and bodywork their task would be simple but from the start they had far more ambitious plans set for the RD. To help offset the often twitchy nature of the RD's handling they would extend the wheelbase by relocating the swingarm pivot rearward an extra three inches. This added length

To complete their newest project the team at Circle K Kustoms will use the remains of two Yamahas, a RD and RZ, to have enough of the main parts needed.

Finding cycles in this condition is not impossible but be sure to check with your state about titling machines assembled from a variety of bits before jumping in feet first.

The selected parts from both bikes are removed then sorted to be sure that all the required hardware is on hand.

Mark Snyder of Circle K Kustom fame smiles as he faces the task of getting the RD motor ready for upgrades and reassembly.

Except for the new bodywork, nearly every bit of required hardware is on display for review so the team can select the chores each needs to accomplish.

The required parts to enhance the motor, including the Moto-Carrera Millennium pipes, are laid out so the crew can do a good inventory.

would also allow them to use the RZ swingarm, adding more stability to the equation. Changing the rear suspension to a Fox gas monoshock would also improve handling while showing off the talents of the crew at Circle K. Adding the triple-trees and front fork from the Yamaha RZ would provide added stiffness and a pair of disc brakes to the front wheel assembly. Braided stainless steel brake lines and a Nissin master cylinder would bring a greater level of sharpness to the braking system and look great while doing so. The RZ hardware would also bring a set of cast wheels to the equation in place of the wire rims found on the RD. Combining that modification to an already lengthy list of upgrades the team set themselves into motion as the clock began to tick away towards the deadline.

Arranging every component neatly on work tables the gang once again ensured that every required component was in house before work began. After confirming the inventory, the first changes were made to the RD350 motor with porting modified for smoother delivery of power along with some '70s black magic raised the horsepower from around 30 to nearly 60. Other alterations needed to be made so the motor could be mated with Banshee reed blocks, Moto-Carrera Millennium exhaust pipes and 32mm round-slide carbs. Enhanced performance was a big part of the improved appearance of their RD as they hoped to achieve a high level of quality to every facet of the build.

Two different seat and tail sections were found and after checking for fit and function the vintage yellow Ducati piece was selected for use due to better alignment with the frame and tank. With plans to lengthen the chassis many careful measurements needed to be taken to achieve the correct geometry to ensure safe performance. Two links were fashioned to provide the extension and would be mounted in place by Kurt's able-bodied hands. Additional reinforcements were made to the frame tubes to support the Ducati seat section and test fitting was done at several stages of that process, assuring that when the time comes to mount the painted bits all will be well. The front fairing required its own set of space frame mounting hardware to connect it to the chassis of the RD and it was also accomplished by Kurt's gifted hands. The engine-turned trim ring that holds the headlight in place was achieved by pounding the original piece into submission with a hard wood form then using a sanding disc in a drill press to apply the final effect.

Next step in the process is to test fit the motor and pipes to check details required for mounting brackets, proper clearance and spacing of other components. Front and rear suspensions can then be placed in position to also check for fit and function. Once all has been approved to fit every piece is once again removed so that the modified frame can be bead-blasted to ensure a clean surface before the paint is applied. Due to the short time frame for this build the paint was applied at night, outside using hand held lamps to illuminate the process. When the paint on the frame has dried it is brought back into the shop for reattachment of the major and minor components. Rick Goldberg was tapped to apply the paint and powder coat to the proper components and the graphics were created and applied by Chris Bottoni. Richard had worked up 100s of options for the chosen graphics and took some diligence to narrow down the selection before making the final choice.

As the last bits of hardware were attached to the frame the final vision of their concept became real. All parties involved were pleased with the results and the RD was greatly received at the Rockerbox show that followed immediately after completion. Kurt, Karl and Robert Schwengel were all a part of the team responsible for getting this project from sketch pad to the show in such short order. I'm certain that any future projects will reach the same heights as the RD and given adequate time who knows what levels of perfection they can reach.

Porting the cylinders takes a skilled hand, but only simple tools, to get more air and fuel in and out of the cylinder. They chose to use a Harry Barlow port map as their guide due.

Removing the outer case of the motor exposes the components within and allows for much easier access for alteration.

Here we see Richard displaying how the finished machine will look when equipped with the high performance expansion chambers and exhaust pipes.

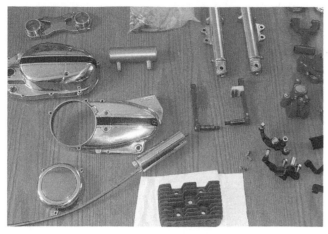

An array of engine and suspension pieces are now laid out to ensure that complete assemblies are on hand and finished for assembly.

Moving the swingarm pivot back, and redesigning the rear suspension required careful planning and multiple mock-up sessions.

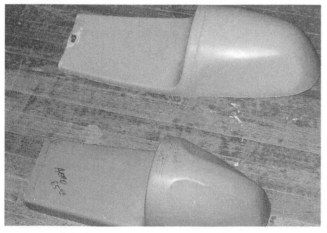

After being checked for fit the yellow section, borrowed from a Ducati, was chosen as it fits better with the fuel tank and chassis layout.

A hand held band saw is used to remove unneeded mounting flanges and tabs from the frame for a cleaner appearance.

An early test fit or mock up. This will be done repeatedly as each segment of the build is completed to be sure that all the parts fit for final assembly.

Kurt shows us the pair of extension flanges he has created that will allow them to move the rear suspension away from its factory position and add length to the revised chassis.

126

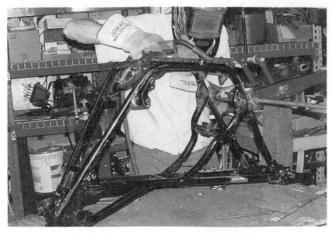

Kurt now welds the extenders into position for a sturdy mounting to the chassis.

Reassembly of the motor is a painstaking task that requires a delicate touch and care to not allow dirt and debris into the mix.

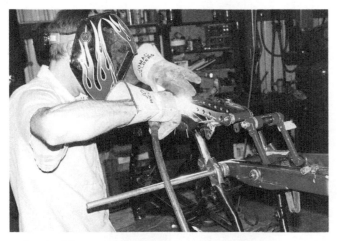

The freshly minted extenders are only one section of the revised single shock rear suspension but when complete will work like a charm.

The rear frame section is cleaned up prior to fabrication and installation of the frame extension.

The welding process can be dramatic but when done properly will deliver a bond between metals that is unbreakable.

With the tail piece sitting in place to ensure everything will fit when they're finished, the new frame extension is tack welded into place.

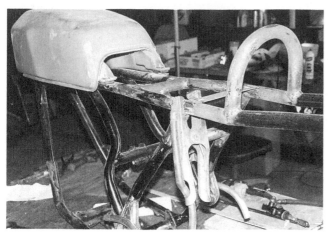

Here's the new hoop of steel welded in place, this loop will support the tail section.

The front forks from the RZ are placed into the triple trees to check for fit and geometry once more before final assembly.

Additional fits and filling in of gaps can now be done since the supporting frame bits have been added providing the permanent locations for each part.

Suspension at both ends is now test fitted along with the correct wheels and tires to ensure function prior to tear down and painting.

Pre-fitting the motor and pipes tells the team where brackets to hold the exhaust in place are needed.

The RD engine is once again placed in the frame so that the carbs and necessary hardware can be tested.

With the carbs in place the rest of the hardware is be mounted to the motor one final time before everything is pulled apart for final paint.

All traces of previous paint, and any rust, are removed before the patining begins to ensure the new paint will adhere to the old Yamaha frame.

Clip-on bars, hand controls and the headlight bucket are also test fitted one more time before the final assembly can start.

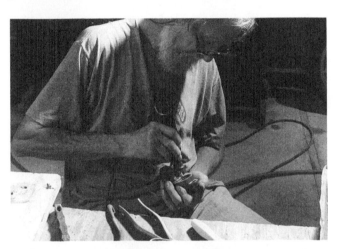

Robert takes his time to remove any excess paint from the bright red brake housings to ensure proper function when they assembled.

With the bodywork in primer the team does one last mock-up before all the parts are sent off for paint and graphics.

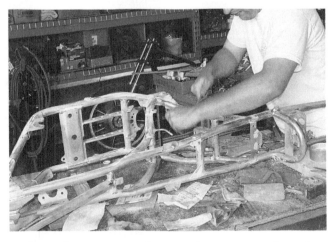

Taking the time to make sure that every nook and cranny of the chassis is free of paint and debris will deliver a better finished paint job.

129

With a fresh coat of black on the frame the engine can go back into place as the final assembly slips into high gear.

The front fairing is now in position and final attention to the wiring harness is addressed at the tail section of the chassis.

The team reviews their efforts before the bodywork is bolted on hiding some of their craftwork.

With less than a day to spare the seat and tail section are attached and the highly revised RD can be taken to the Rockerbox show in Milwaukee for its debut.

This particular Cafe fairing uses a plexiglass cover over the headlight.

What started as a Ducati tail section now graces the rear end of this hybrid Yamaha, complete with a hand-stitched seat.

A close up view of the custom single-shock rear suspension installation. Note the engine detailing, and the mounting of the rear brake master cylinder.

Chapter Ten

Build #2

Honda CB200 Café Conversion

Richard Weslow, his friends and brother, all share a long standing enthusiasm for the motorcycle world. Having ridden and worked on numerous cycles in the past, Richard thought he'd try his hand at building a Café Racer since he could sense that segment of the hobby was growing at a fever pitch. Seeing all the exposure the trend is getting he figured it was one of the best times to complete a project in that vein while contacts and parts were get-

With final assembly complete we can view the results of Richard's dreams and his friends' talents and efforts.

ting easier to find every day. His ambition was also fired by his meeting with Mark and Linda Wilsmore in 2008. They have been the owners of the Ace Café in London since they purchased the property about a decade ago. Speaking with them at the Milwaukee Rockerbox event was the perfect storm of inspiration for Richard and his pals to step up to the Café Racer table. Living fairly close to Milwaukee he has years of experience with the Harley riding crowd and all the related excitement. Although it wasn't a genre he cared to join, he still wanted a sporty set of two-wheels under his butt. Once the fire was lit the gang decided on three different builds they would achieve with the trio falling squarely in the Café Racer department, while bringing their own personal creativity to the machines.

After he learned of the fame and notoriety of the Ace Café in London - with its roots leading all the way back to the 1960s making it THE place to attend weekend events and to exchange information about your current ride or future build. Taking all of this into account he set out to try his hand at constructing a nimble yet entertaining machine for the Café Racer crowd. Additional research led him to the popularity and widespread availability of the Honda CB200 models. Sold in the USA from 1974 through 1976 the versatile cycle was not large or powerful but provided riders a dependable platform to learn, commute or simply enjoy. The overhead cam, parallel twin motor displaced 198cc and delivered a

pleasant amount of power without intimidating the rider. He also saw the familiar profile that the vertical twin motor and tank design of the CB200 shared with the early versions of the Café Racer.

Locating a donor machine was fairly simple as their availability in nearly every state of condition can be found through traditional or modern electronic shopping venues. Once he had located a fairly complete CB200 the entire machine was stripped down to the bare frame and work began on converting it to a modern Café Racer for the street. Turning to his friend Kurt for assistance, Richard knew he'd get strong guidance along with a high level of ability as he asked Kurt to lend his vast amount of experience to the conversion. Before any actual work began on the rebuild the team spent a lot of time discussing, sketching and planning out the required steps to bring the beat up CB200 to a new level of glamour. After every facet of the conversion had been discussed and agreed upon, work was set into motion.

With the frame stripped of all components, Kurt can now review the steps required to take the project to completion.

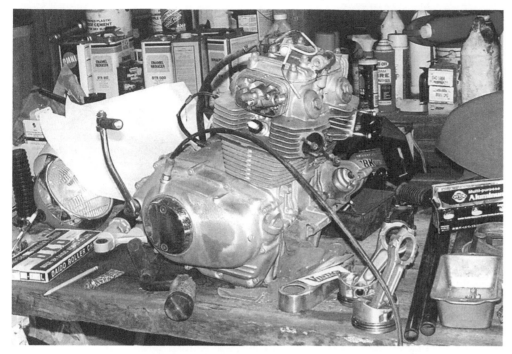

Most of the needed parts can now be laid out to assure all are in place and additional checks can be made for condition and needed changes.

One of the most dramatic changes to be made to the motor would be the addition of a pair of velocity stacks in lieu of the plastic factory airbox. Typically making this change requires a screwdriver and little more, but the size of the CB200 frame and its layout would mean a few extra steps to accomplish the task. When placing the stacks on the carbs there was an immediate issue of the primary frame upright hampering their installation. To address this concern Kurt cut two semi-circles from the upright to allow enough space for the stacks.

Not wanting to leave a large amount of steel missing from the strategic section of the chassis Kurt used two small sections of steel pipe to fill the gap while leaving the required semi-circles in the frame. By welding and grinding these small segments of steel into place the result looks like a factory procedure while allowing the much cooler velocity stacks a place to live.

Another removal from the factory design was a majority of the exhaust system. They didn't want the weight and complexity of the original exhaust to hamper the look and sound

Placing the sheet metal and fiberglass components onto the frame allows the gang to determine what brackets will need to be fabricated and what can be removed from the chassis.

of their creation so the down tubes of the system were cut off about 16 inches from the motor. This was also decided as they tried to add the feel of a Spitfire fighter from WW II to the mix in keeping with the Ace Café motif. By using a pair of resonators from a Volkswagen Bug engine they could achieve a smaller and lighter exhaust and save a lot of nonsense hanging off of the machine. Attaching the

With the sections of the Honda frame removed, Kurt welds into place two beefier lengths of tube that will offer support for the new tail section.

VW sections to the remaining exhaust tubes would mean a weld in a very obvious spot. The fabrication also left the pipes dangling without support. To support the pipes, and hide the welded seam, the crew used an old set of connecting rods from a Briggs and Stratton motor. By attaching the small end to the frame, the big end neatly wrapped around the pipe. This little alteration is one of the great details found on this CB200 as it went from stock to Café Racer.

It was also decided to change the mounting points of the rear shocks. To achieve this a "V" was cut into each leg of the swingarm at the top section of flange. They could have simply welded the rear shocks onto the edge of the steel flange but by adding the "V" cut it would double the space

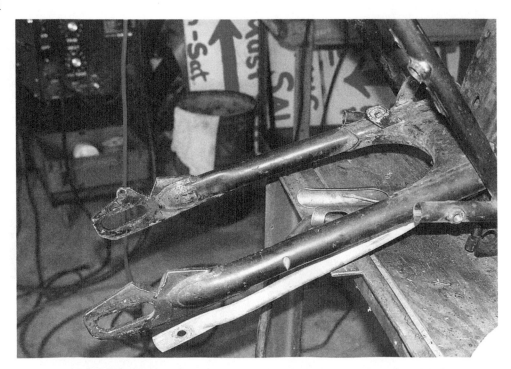

A pair of "V" notches has been cut into the swingarm to provide added strength when the new brackets are welded into place.

A section of smaller diameter tubing has been formed to fit between the new rear sections of tubing to support other aspects of the revised chassis.

To make room for the velocity stacks, the vertical frame support had to be cut out and then reinforced.

provided to weld the new brackets into place. Small yet vital changes like this were one of the hallmarks of Kurt's abilities and why Richard wanted his expertise and guidance. New sections were formed and welded to the frame to mount the Café Racer seat and tail section and unnecessary flanges and mounting tabs were then removed from the chassis for a tidier appearance and a modicum of weight savings.

With all of the modifications completed on the frame it was sprayed with primer before applying the final black finish. The chain guard was drilled with accent holes that were then chamfered to deliver a more finished appearance. The section of tube holding the tail light in place is actually rigid although it snakes gracefully through the frame tubes. This method provided a flowing look while providing adequate support for the stop light and license plate.

After reviewing a variety of options for paint and graphics the green base color was chosen, accented with the black and white checkerboard pattern and Ace Café logos. Small, circular badges of the British military

Here we can see that the two lengths of new frame section have been sliced at an angle and covered with new plates of steel. Note the new support piece for the tail section, now welded in place.

were added to the front headlight ears along with decorative coins on the rear section for added flair. The majority of the suspension, brakes, wheels and tires were left in stock condition to save money and to keep their first Café Racer project simple. Once the experience in the field was gained more challenging and difficult choices would be taken in their subsequent projects.

The finished machine is compact. Wearing the Café seat and tail piece along with the clubman bars gives it all the required visual clues of a true Café Racer. Due to the high degree of assistance from friends and the low cost of parts and the donor cycle, this entire project came in under their estimated budget - which helped make the end result even more satisfying.

After painting the tank, the area to be painted with the Ace Cafe logo needs to be taped off and sanded.

Two of the team members toil away at forming another fresh segment of required sheet metal to be attached to the frame.

Put on display at a local event, the Ace Café CB200 gets rave reviews and plenty of attention during its debut showing.

Builder Interview:

In my travels through the world of all things mechanical I have often stumbled into a person who possesses an innate ability to grasp how things function and how to improve that function. Like a professional athlete these folks are born with the skills and are able to cultivate them into a highly functioning talent. My wanderings in the Café Racer universe exposed me to another of these people and Kurt Schwengel is the most recent of my discoveries. Kurt's fellow associate Richard Weslow refers to him as "the world's greatest shop teacher" as he has witnessed Kurt work his magic on a variety of projects. As I spoke with Kurt about the 2 cycles they built for this book his views only shed a brighter light on how skilled he is at achieving success regardless of the challenges he faces.

Tell us a little about your background and how you became engaged in the world of building motorcycles.

I have been a small engine mechanic for more than 25 years and discovered an early interest in how things worked when I was younger. After meeting Richard many years ago I found myself being drawn into the two-wheeled arena and the new paths that were available.

Have all of your motorcycle projects been in the Café Racer mold?

My early attraction was to anything with wheels and once I began spending time

Kurt Schwengel (right) and Richard Weslow (left) are seen at the big Rockerbox event in Wisconsin showing off their latest Café Racer to an enthusiastic crowd.

Kurt Schwengel

with Richard I found myself more deeply immersed in the cycle arena. We have built Café Racers, speed trackers and a bobber so far and we have a few more projects on the drawing board now.

What's your favorite aspect of the Café Racer mold?

The simplicity of a true Café Racer makes them very approachable and brings almost immediate gratification versus building a custom car. The basic layout of a Café Racer can also be achieved with a minimum of space and tools making it more accessible to garage builders everywhere.

What sort of shop and tools would a person need to build a Café Racer of their own?

In the early days of the Café Racer we saw young guys utilizing whatever hardware they could find. With only the most rudimentary tools they could create a unique machine. Although there are far more choices today regarding hardware and options the basic assembly can still be done while keeping things simple.

In terms of skills, what level of talent does a person need to do an at-home build?

Much of that would depend on the complexity of the project and a person's aptitude in the mechanical field. If welding and metal working are part of the design they'd need to be sure they had access and talents to suit those goals.

Are there any segments of a build that would be better if farmed out?

Again that would depend on a person's ambitions and skills. If machining is required or welding finding an outside source for those tasks would deliver better results in most cases unless you have a CNC machine and top-grade welding equipment at your fingertips. There can be a whole lot of voodoo in achieving certain tasks and some may be better suited to a skilled tradesman.

Any suggestions for a good starting point for a home builder?

I always suggest you begin with a cycle that already runs and rides well. By eliminating mechanical issues before you begin it removes a high level of frustration that can arise when the engine stops functioning. More common machines also require fewer exotic bits to maintain so I'd say stay within the range of readily available cycles to start.

Any other tips for the first time builder?

I would again suggest they begin with a working machine and be sure to do plenty of advance planning before taking a new creation under your wings. Some are resistant to cutting up a vintage machine in good shape so decide the level of comfort before hacking into a hard-to-replace piece of metal. Plan the build in advance as best you can to avoid complications down the road. Research and bench planning will save you lots of aggravation later in the process.

Are there mistakes a beginner can avoid?

By making changes that remain within your own set of skills you'll avoid some really big issues. Don't make any drastic alterations unless you are sure you can correct them if required. Cutting a fuel tank in two is easy but welding it back together is not easy at all. As I mentioned before, planning the build in advance will help even a first-timer to avoid trouble as things progress.

Is there more you'd like to add?

From my standpoint I suggest you organize the build in stages. Welding, mechanical and electric work needs to be completed before moving to the finishing stages unless you like to risk damaging freshly painted or polished components. Be sure new parts will work with the existing layout. A better exhaust system might look and sound great, but if it interferes with the kick-start lever you are going to regret your selection Allow time for snags in the process as many will pop up without notice no matter how much you've planned. Delays in getting parts can also wreak havoc with the process so do your best to use local or reliable sources for parts and services.

After completing the changes, the critical sections are masked off prior to application of the first layer of primer. Keeping the bearing surfaces free of paint will ensure safe operation once assembly is complete.

Positioned on the work table the guys now arrange the required brackets and bolts that will be installed onto the frame.

With the primer now complete the frame can be taken out to be painted in its final hue of black. You can see the flowing tail light bracket extending from the rear section.

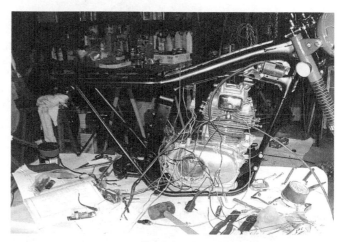

Bolting the engine in place, the team begins installing the wiring harness that will bring life to the electrical components of the final product.

Now coated with gleaming black paint the chassis can be taken to the next step of reassembly.

The next pieces to be bolted in place are the front forks, rear swingarm, suspension and wheel. Rear brakes and related brackets are also put in position as the final steps of assembly grow near.

The seat and rear tail section can now be checked for proper alignment one last time as the final steps of the project come together.

The front wheel and brakes, headlight bucket and fuel tank go into position along with the front fender, allowing us our first glimpse of the overall graphics theme.

HOW TO BUILD AN OLD SKOOL BOBBER

Kevin lays out the basics of bike building, starting first with the ideal components: which engine, which frame, and the differences in the various years. Next, things to watch out for when buying old parts, and how to fix the parts you do buy. Additional chapters describe brake systems, both early and late, tires and wheels, and frame geometry. Four complete start-to-fin-ish bike assemblies round out this hands-on book.

You don't need a lot of money and you don't need a catalog filled with shiny billet parts. You just need an engine and a frame, the burning desire to build a bike that's truly your own, and a copy of Kevin's new book: How to Build an Old Skool Bobber, second edition.

| Thirteen Chapters | 144 Pages | $27.95 | Over 350 photos, 100% color |

HOW TO BUILD A CHEAP CHOPPER

Choppers don't have to cost $30,000. In fact, a chopper built from the right parts can be assembled for as little as $5,000. How to Build a Cheap Chopper documents the construction of 4 inexpensive choppers with complete start-to-finish sequences photographed in the shops of Donnie Smith, Brian Klock and Dave Perewitz.

Least expensive is the metric chopper, based on a Japanese 4-cylinder engine and transmission installed in a hardtail frame. Next up, price wise, are 2 bikes built using Buell/Sportster drivetrains. The recipe here is simple; combine one used Buell or Sportster with a hardtail frame for an almost instant chopper. The big twin chopper is the least cheap of the 4, yet it's still far less expensive than most bikes built today.

| Eleven Chapters | 144 Pages | $27.95 | Over 300 photos, 100% color |

KOSMOSKI'S NEW KUSTOM PAINTING SECRETS

Jon starts with the basics: how to set up a shop, pick a compressor, and prepare the metal. Next comes a thorough discussion of modern paint: What it is, how it's made and which type is best suited to custom paintwork.

How to pick, adjust and use spray guns makes up the next section in Jon's new book. As Jon explains, "you need to have the gun adjusted properly, and the way to do that is with test panels done before you start the paint job." The test panels included in the book show a good and bad pattern, and how to adjust a gun that's putting out a flawed pattern.

No how-to-paint would be complete without at least two, start-to-finish paint jobs. Kosmoski's New Kustom Painting Secrets contains both a hot rod and a motorcycle paint job.

| Eight Chapters | 144 Pages | $27.95 | Over 400 photos, 100% color |

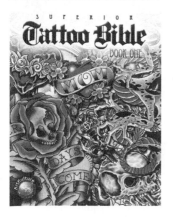

TATTOO BIBLE BOOK ONE

Whether you are preparing for your first tattoo or your twenty-seventh, you need artwork and designs that are just-right. Tattoo Bible, authored by Superior Tattoo, provides well over 500 pieces of unique flash art - flash never before compiled into one single book.

While most tattoo books available today concentrate on one specific genre, this Tattoo Bible covers many different genres and the ideas are end-less. This is not just a book to add to your collection - this is your collection. You can combine different pieces of art from within the book, or just take them as is. This book is for you and your imagination to do with as you wish.

Published by ArtKulture, an imprint of Wolfgang Publications, with images that are both striking and very useful to both the tattoo shop, and the tattoo aficionado.

| Ten Chapters | 144 Pages | $27.95 | Over 400 photos, 100% color |

Wolfgang Publication Titles

For a current list visit our website at www.wolfpub.com

ILLUSTRATED HISTORY

Ultimate Triumph Collection	$49.95

BIKER BASICS

Custom Bike Building Basics	$24.95
Custom Bike Building ADVANCED	$24.95
Sportster/Buell Engine Hop-Up Guide	$24.95
Sheet Metal Fabrication Basics	$24.95

COMPOSITE GARAGE

Composite Materials Handbook #1	$27.95
Composite Materials Handbook #2	$27.95
Composite Materials Handbook #3	$27.95

HOT ROD BASICS

Hot Rod Wiring	$27.95
How to Chop Tops	$24.95
How to Air Condition Your Hot Rod	$24.95

MOTORCYCLE RESTORATION SERIES

Triumph Restoration - Unit 650cc	$29.95
Triumph MC Restoration Pre-Unit	$29.95

CUSTOM BUILDER SERIES

How to Build A Café Racer	$27.95
Advanced Custom Motorcycle Wiring - Revised	$27.95
How to Build an Old Skool Bobber Sec Ed	$27.95
How To Build The Ultimate V-Twin Motorcycle	$24.95
Advanced Custom Motorcycle Assembly & Fabrication	$27.95
Advanced Custom Motorcycle Chassis	$27.95
How to Build a Cheap Chopper	$27.95
How to Build a Chopper	$27.95

SHEET METAL

Advanced Sheet Metal Fabrication	$27.95
Ultimate Sheet Metal Fabrication	$24.95
Sheet Metal Bible	$29.95

AIR SKOOL SKILLS

Airbrush Bible	$29.95
How Airbrushes Work	$24.95

PAINT EXPERT

How To Airbrush, Pinstripe & Goldleaf	$27.95
Kosmoski's New Kustom Painting Secrets	$27.95
Advanced Custom Motorcycle Painting	$27.95
Pro Pinstripe Techniques	$27.95
Advanced Pinstripe Art	$27.95

TATTOO U Series

Into The Skin The Ultimate Tattoo Sourcebook	$34.95
Tattoo Sketch Book	$32.95
American Tattoos	$27.95
Tattoo - From Idea to Ink	$27.95
Advanced Tattoo Art	$27.95
Tattoo Bible Book One	$27.95
Tattoo Bible Book Two	$27.95
Tattoo Bible Book Three	$27.95

NOTEWORTHY

American Police Motorcycles - Revised	$24.95
Guitar Building Basics Acoustic Assembly at Home	$27.95

LIFESTYLE

Bean're — Motorcycle Nomad	$18.95
The Colorful World of Tattoo Models	$34.95

Source Guide

Air-Tech Streamlining
Vista, CA
www.airtech-streamlining.com
760-598-3366

Alliance Power Sports
www.alliancepowersports.com
951-361-9000

Analog Motorcycles
Gurnee, IL
www.analogmotorcycless.com
analogmotorcycles@gmail.com

Bridge City Cycles
Portland, OR
www.bridgecitycycles.com
503-284-1503

British Customs
www.british-customs.com
877-999-BRIT

Buchanan's Spoke and Rim, Inc.
www.buchananspokes.com
626-969-4655

Circle K Kustoms
Milwaukee, WI
262-593-2896

Clubman Racing Accessories
Fairfield, CT
www.clubmanracing.com
203-261-9574

Coating Specialties
South Chicago Heights, IL
www.coatingspecialties.com
708-754-3311

Colorado Norton Works
www.coloradonortonworks.com

Dennis Kirk
www.denniskirk.com/caferacer
800-970-3808

Dime City Cycles
Largo, FL
www.dimecitycycles.com
888-555-1212

Dobeck Performance
Belgrade, MT
www.dobeckperformance.com
406-388-2377

DP Customs
New River, AZ
www.dpcustomcycles.com
623-695-1495

Economy Cycle
Winthrop Harbor, IL
www.economycycle.com
224-430-7971

Evan Wilcox
Ukiah, CA
www.wilcoxmetal.com
707-467-3993

Fast From The Past
www.fastfromthepast.com

Flatland Custom Cycles, Inc. /
GAZI Suspension
Arlington Heights, IL
www.gazisuspension.com
847-253-6922

Framecrafters
Union, IL
www.framecrafters.com
815-923-4537

Gasket King
www.gasketking.com
702-232-8172

Gustafsson Plastics, Inc.
St. Augustine, FL
www.bikescreen.com
888-824-3443

Hagon Shocks
San Marcos, CA
www.hagonshocksusa.com
760-308-8124

Heidenau Tires
www.heidenauusa.com
408-295-3004

Hotwing Glass
www.hotwingglass.com
352-447-4720

JC-PakBikes
Altadena, CA
www.jcpakbikes.com
626-794-6439

Joker Machine
www.jokermachine.com
909-596-9690

Ken's British Classics
www.kensbritishclassics.com
847-746-3613

KOSO North America
Canada
www.kosonorthamerica.com
877-777-0604

Legendary-Motorcycles.com
www.legendary-motorcycles.com
239-404-3600

MCC (Motor Cycle Center)
Villa Park, IL
www.TeamMCC.com
630-782-2010

Moto-Scoot
Milwaukee, WI
www.moto-scoot.net
414-272-6680

Moto-Services.net
www.moto-services.net
909-273-4985

Rabers Parts Mart, Inc.
San Jose, CA
www.rabers.com
408-998-4495

Race Tech Suspension
www.racetech.com
951-279-6655

Radiantz L.E.D. Lighting
Brookings, OR
www.radiantz.com
877-469-4241

Rizoma USA
Beverly Hills, CA
www.rizoma.com
877-749-6621

Roland Sands Design
www.rolandsands.com

Route 31 Hot Rods
McHenry, IL
www.route31hotrods.com
815-759-2277

Royal Enfield
www.royalenfieldusa.com

Steadfast Cycles
www.steadfastcycles.com
661-877-7911
661-252-5822

StreetFighters, Inc.
Glendale, AZ
www.streetfightersinc.com
623-581-1994

Sudco International Corp.
Compton, CA
www.sudco.com
310-637-8330

Syds Cycles, Inc.
St. Petersburg, FL
sydscycles@aol.com
727-522-3333

Union Motorcycle Classics
www.unionmotorcycle.com

VarnHagen Metalworks
www.vhmetalworks.com
217-440-8645

Vintage Smoke
www.vintagesmoke.com

Walneck's Classic Cycle Trader
866-880-3666

YSS Suspension
Manalapan, NJ
www.yssusa.com

Zero Gravity Racing
Camarillo, CA
www.ZeroGravity-Racing.com
805-388-8803

CPSIA information can be obtained at www.ICGtesting.com
Printed in the USA
LVOW020645070513

332612LV00004B/4/P

$27⁹⁵ U.S.

How To Build A
Café Racer

What's old is new again, and the newest trend on the block is Café Racers. Written by well-known motorcycle and automotive author Doug Mitchel, *How to Build a Café Racer* starts with the history lesson. And though those first bikes were build in the UK for racing from café to café, the current rage for Café Racers has definitely spread to the US.

Converting a stock motorcycle to a Café Racer requires more than a fairing and a few decals. Doug starts the book with a chapter on planning. Choosing an appropriate bike comes next, followed by chapters that detail the modifications that will likely be embraced by anyone converting a stocker to a rocker. From shocks and tires to engine modifications, Doug's book lays out each type of modification, and how it's best carried through.

The center of the book holds a gallery of finished bikes. These are not just Triumphs or Nortons, but nearly every brand imaginable from Japan, Italy, the UK and Germany.

The final chapters include two, start-to-finish Café builds. This is the chance for the reader to see how professional shops take a stock Honda, Triumph or Ducati and convert it into a fast, sexy and functional Café Racer, ready to race from café to café on Saturday night, or around the race track on Sunday afternoon.

Printed in U.S.A.
Published by:

Wolfgang
Publications

PO Box 223 • Stillwater, MN 55082
www.wolfpub.com

ISBN 978-1-935828-73-0

90000

9 781935 828730

T4-ASI-971